Get To The Core of Healthy Fibromyalgia Cooking

ISBN 1-4196-1157-7

To order additional copies, please contact us.
BookSurge, LLC
www.booksurge.com
1-866-308-6235
orders@booksurge.com

Table of Contents

Introduction

Learning How to Cook When You Have Fibromyalgia

Learning how to cook when you have fibromyalgia is really not that difficult. It is a matter of using the correct ingredients that are helpful with your diet and nutrition. It is learning what ingredients might be "trigger foods" and replacing them with healthier and safe choices. I will teach you about different foods, good and bad. I will show you ways to eat and drink to boost your energy levels for a more dynamic, active lifestyle. There are foods that can make a dramatic improvement in the way you feel, without sacrificing taste or ease of preparation. They are all here in this cookbook for you to utilize. So, pick out some of the recipes that you just cannot resist and try them. I guarantee you that you will be happy with your selections and this healthy diet and nutritional way of cooking will benefit your health and well being for life.

This book is dedicated to the encouragement of my family and friends to pursue healthier living with fibromyalgia. Without them, I would still be in the fibromyalgia rut. With their help, I feel great and look forward to living life to the fullest!

Beverages

Apple Smoothie

Ingredients:
3 cups cold apple cider
2 bananas
1 small carton plain yogurt

Directions:
Blend in blender and chill. Serve in cold glasses

Makes 2 to 3 servings

Healthy Fruit Smoothie

Ingredients:
½ cup fruit juice, unsweetened
1 apple, peeled and cut into small pieces
½ cup frozen peaches
½ cup frozen cherries
1 small container plain yogurt

Directions:
Combine fruit juice, peeled and cut apple, frozen peaches, frozen cherries, and yogurt in blender. Blend until smooth. Pour into glasses. Decorate with a maraschino cherry or a peach slice.

Makes 2-3 servings

Mango and Banana Smoothie

Ingredients:
1 mango, peeled, pitted, and coarsely chopped
1 banana, peeled and cut into several pieces
One 8-ounce container vanilla yogurt
½ cup orange juice
Ice, optional

Directions:
Combine all the ingredients except optional ice in a food processor or blender and process until smoothly puréed. Serve at once in tall glasses, over ice if desired.

Makes 2 servings

Mango-Strawberry Smoothie

Ingredients:
1 mango, peeled, pitted, and coarsely chopped
1 cup fresh strawberries
One 8-ounce container vanilla yogurt
½ cup orange juice
Ice, optional

Directions:
Combine mango, strawberries, vanilla yogurt, and orange juice in a food processor or blender and process until smoothly puréed. Serve at once in tall glasses, over ice if desired.

Makes 2 servings

Raspberry Cream Smoothie

Ingredients:
1 cup orange juice
1 cup raspberry yogurt
1 cup vanilla frozen yogurt
½ frozen banana (chunks)
1½ cup frozen raspberries

Directions:
Mix all ingredients in a blender or smoothie machine putting liquid and soft ingredients in first. Blend until smooth. Serve cold.

Makes 2 large smoothies or 4 small smoothies

Strawberry Banana Supreme Smoothie

Ingredients:
1 cup strawberry nectar or apple juice
1 cup milk
1 frozen banana
1½ cups frozen strawberries
1 cup strawberry yogurt

Directions:
Mix all ingredients in a blender or smoothie machine. Put all soft ingredients in first. Blend until smooth. Serve cold.

Makes 2 large smoothies or 4 small smoothies

Sunshine Smoothie

Ingredients:
2 cups blackberries, fresh or frozen
2 cups raspberries, fresh or frozen
2 cups sliced fresh strawberries
2 large ripe bananas, thinly sliced

Individual smoothies add:
1 cup unsweetened apple juice
¼ teaspoon vanilla extract

Directions:
Combine the blackberries, raspberries, strawberries, and bananas in a large, resealable plastic bag and freeze overnight. The fruit will keep in the freezer for up to 4 months.

To make one smoothie, scoop 1 cup of the fruit mixture into the blender. Add the apple juice and vanilla and blend in blender until smooth.

Makes 8 servings of fruit mixture to make 8 smoothies

Condiments, Dips, Salad Dressings, Sauces and Spreads

Homemade Ketchup

Ingredients
1 can (8 ounces) tomato sauce
¾ cup tomato paste
2 tablespoons xylitol (sugar) (see glossary for definition)
2 teaspoons onion powder
2 teaspoons soy sauce
½ teaspoon ground cloves
½ teaspoon ground allspice
1½ tablespoons malt vinegar

Directions:
In a large saucepan over medium heat, combine the tomato sauce, tomato paste, xylitol, onion powder, soy sauce, cloves, allspice, and vinegar. Simmer for 5 minutes. Refrigerate until serving. (Keeps covered and sealed in refrigerator for one week.)

Makes about 1 cup

Homemade Mayonnaise

Ingredients:
4 large garlic cloves
¼ cup eggs (1 egg)
1-2 tablespoons lemon juice
¼ teaspoon salt
¾ cup olive oil

Directions:
In a blender, combine garlic, egg, lemon juice, and salt. Blend 5 seconds; gradually add oil in thin steady stream. Pour mixture into a sealed, covered container and refrigerate up to 3 days.

Makes approximately 1 cup

Light Cheese Dip

Ingredients:
1 cup cottage cheese
¼ cup light cream cheese
1 teaspoon salt-free seasoning
2 tablespoons fresh parsley or fresh dill, minced

Directions:
Combine all of the ingredients in a food processor or blender. Process until smoothly puréed. Transfer to a serving bowl. Cover and refrigerate until needed or serve at once.

Makes 6 to 8 servings

Fruit Dip

Ingredients:
¼ cup xylitol (sugar) (see glossary for definition)
3 tablespoons cinnamon
2 tablespoons dried lemon or orange peel, ground
1 teaspoon allspice
1 teaspoon cloves
½ teaspoon nutmeg

Directions:
Combine all the ingredients in a small bowl and store, tightly covered, up to 2 months. Sprinkle one tablespoon on fresh apples, strawberries, pears, etc.

Makes 8 servings

Peanut Dip

Ingredients:
2 cups chopped unsalted roasted peanuts
½ cup plain yogurt
¼ teaspoon lemon peel, finely grated
Salt to taste

Directions:
In a blender or food processor, combine the peanuts, yogurt, lemon peel, and salt to taste, and process until smooth.

Makes 2½ cups

Tomato Salsa

Ingredients:
1 large lime
1½ pounds ripe tomatoes (3 large tomatoes), chopped
½ small red onion, finely chopped
1 small jalapeño chili, seeded and minced
¾ teaspoon salt
¼ teaspoon black pepper

Directions:
From the lime, grate ½ teaspoon peel and squeeze 2 tablespoons juice. In a medium bowl, gently stir lime peel, lime juice, tomatoes, onion, jalapeño, salt, and pepper until well mixed. Cover and refrigerate at least 1 hour to blend flavors or up to 2 days.

Makes about 3 cups

Yogurt Cheese Cucumber Dip

Ingredients:
2 cups plain yogurt
1 cucumber, grated
½ cup fresh lemon juice
2 cloves garlic, minced
1 tablespoon fresh dill, chopped

Directions:
Line a strainer or sieve with a double layer of cheesecloth and place it over a bowl. Spoon in the yogurt and tie the corners of the cheesecloth together. Let it drain in the refrigerator overnight. Do not allow the strainer to touch the liquid. Squeeze the yogurt gently and remove it from the cheesecloth. Discard the liquid.

Squeeze the cucumber in a towel to remove moisture.

In a large bowl, combine the cucumber, yogurt cheese, lemon juice, and garlic. Sprinkle with the dill.

Makes 1 cup

Apricot Dressing

Ingredients:
⅓ cup apricot nectar
3 tablespoons dried apricots, minced
3 tablespoons balsamic vinegar
3 tablespoons fresh parsley, coarsely chopped
2 tablespoons olive oil
2 teaspoons garlic, minced
2 teaspoons dry mustard
1 teaspoon xylitol (sugar) (see glossary for definition)
Salt and pepper to taste

Directions:
Whisk apricot nectar, apricots, vinegar, parsley, oil, garlic, mustard, xylitol, salt and pepper in a bowl.

Makes about ¾ cup

Cucumber & Sesame Seed Dressing

Ingredients:
1 cup cider vinegar
1 cup water
2 tablespoons lemon juice, fresh
¼ cup sesame seeds
½ cucumber, seeded and cut into cubes
1 onion, cut into cubes
1 clove garlic, chopped
½ teaspoon dried dill
¼ teaspoon salt
½ teaspoon xylitol (sugar) (see glossary for definition)

Directions:
Preheat the oven to 350°F. Spread the sesame seed out on a small baking pan, and bake, stirring frequently, for 10 to 20 minutes, or until the seeds are lightly toasted. Set aside to cool.

Place the cooled seeds and the remaining ingredients in a food processor or blender, and purée for 2 minutes, or until the mixture is smooth and creamy.

Use immediately or place in a tight lid container for up to 5 days in the refrigerator.

Makes 3 cups

Honey Lime Vinaigrette

Ingredients:
⅓ cup fresh lime juice (2 to 3 limes)
4 teaspoons honey
1 tablespoon rice vinegar
⅛ teaspoon salt

Directions:
In a small bowl, with a wire whisk, mix lime juice, honey, vinegar, and salt until blended. Cover and refrigerate up to 3 days.

Makes approximately ½ cup

Honey Mustard Dressing

Ingredients:
½ cup yogurt
½ cup mayonnaise (see recipe in this section)
2 tablespoons lemon juice
1 teapoon dry mustard
¼ cup honey

Directions:
In a small bowl, combine all of the ingredients and blend well. Refrigerate.

Makes approximately 1 cup

Warm Maple Dressing

Ingredients:
2 teaspoons olive oil
1 shallot, finely chopped
¼ cup vinegar
2 tablespoons pure maple syrup
Salt and pepper to taste

Directions:
Heat olive oil in a small skillet over medium-low heat. Add shallot and cook, stirring, until softened, about 4 minutes. Add vinegar and maple syrup and bring to a boil. Season with salt and pepper.

Immediately pour dressing over salad. Toss well.

Makes approximately 4 servings

Orange-Ginger Dressing

Ingredients:
½ cup rice vinegar
½ cup orange juice
½ teaspoon fresh ginger, peeled and grated
½ teaspoon soy sauce
⅛ teaspoon sesame oil

Directions:
In a small bowl, with a wire whisk, mix vinegar, orange juice, ginger, soy sauce, and sesame oil until blended. Cover and refrigerate up to 5 days.

Makes approximately 1 cup

Tomato Dressing

Ingredients:
4 fluid ounces tomato juice
1 clove garlic, crushed
2 tablespoons lemon juice
1 tablespoon soy sauce
1 teaspoon honey
2 tablespoons chives, chopped
salt and pepper to taste

Directions:
Mix all the ingredients into a screw top jar and shake vigorously until well mixed

Makes approximately ½ cup

Creamy Ranch Dressing

Ingredients:
¾ cup plain yogurt
¼ cup mayonnaise (see recipe in this section)
1 green onion, minced
1 tablespoon cider vinegar
2 teaspoons Dijon mustard
¼ teaspoon dried thyme
¼ teaspoon coarsely ground black pepper

Directions:
In a small bowl, with a wire whisk, mix yogurt, mayonnaise, green onion, vinegar, mustard, thyme, and pepper until blended. Cover and refrigerate up to 5 days.

Makes approximately 1 cup

Homemade Barbeque Sauce

Ingredients:
1 cup (8 ounces) tomato sauce
2 tablespoons white vinegar
1 teaspoon Worcestershire sauce
1 teaspoon mustard powder
1 teaspoon dried parsley
¼ teaspoon salt
⅛ teaspoon black pepper
⅛ teaspoon garlic powder

Directions:
In a container that can be resealed, combine the tomato sauce, vinegar, Worcestershire sauce, mustard powder, parsley, salt, pepper, and garlic powder. Blend together until smooth. (Keeps covered and sealed in the refrigerator for 1 week.)

Makes about 1 cup

Fresh Berry Sauce

Ingredients:
2 cups fresh berries (strawberries, blueberries, raspberries, or any combination)
½ cup apple juice
¼ cup cold water
2 teaspoons cornstarch
1 tablespoon xylitol (sugar) (see glossary for definition)

Directions:
Wash the berries well. Small berries do not need to be cut up. Larger berries like strawberries should be cut into smaller pieces.

Combine the berries in a medium size saucepan with the apple juice. Bring to a simmer, cover, and cook gently until all the berries have softened and burst, 5 to 10 minutes.

Dissolve the cornstarch and xylitol in ¼ cup cold water. Stir slowly into the berry mixture and simmer until it has thickened, about 1 minute. Let cool to room temperature before serving.

Makes 6 servings

Freezer Tomato Sauce

Ingredients:
¼ cup canola oil
1 large white onion, minced
2 cloves garlic, minced
6 cans (1 pound each) whole peeled tomatoes
4 stalks celery, finely chopped
1 small green bell pepper, finely chopped
1 medium carrot, finely grated
1 teaspoon dried thyme
2 tablespoons dried oregano
1 teaspoon dried basil
2 teaspoons xylitol (sugar) (see glossary for definition)
1 large bay leaf
1 tablespoon salt
1 teaspoon black pepper
1 can tomato paste

Directions:
Place the oil in a 5-6 quart kettle over medium heat. Add the onion, and cook, stirring often, until the onion is soft, but not brown. Add the garlic, and continue to cook for one minute.

Place the tomatoes, celery, green pepper, and carrot in a blender or food processor, and blend on purée for about 1 minute, or until the tomatoes are well mashed.

Add the tomato mixture and all of the remaining ingredients to the onion mixture. Mix well. Reduce the heat to low, and simmer the sauce uncovered for 2 to 3 hours, stirring every 25-30 minutes.

Remove from the heat and throw away the bay leaf. Taste and adjust the seasoning if necessary, adding tomato paste. Use immediately or cool to room temperature and transfer to containers with sealed lids. Store in the refrigerator for up to 5 days or freeze for up to 3 months.

Makes 12 cups

Cheese Garlic & Herb Pâté

Ingredients:
½ ounce butter
1 clove garlic, crushed
3 green onions, chopped finely
4½ ounces ricotta cheese (any soft cheese of your choice)
2 tablespoons fresh parsley, oregano and basil, chopped and mixed
6 ounces cheddar cheese, grated finely
4–6 slices spelt bread (see bread section for recipe)
pepper to taste
mixed salad leaves and cherry tomatoes to serve on
paprika to garnish

Directions:
Melt the butter in a small frying pan and gently fry the garlic and chopped green onions together for 3 to 4 minutes, until softened. Allow to cool.

Beat the soft cheese in a bowl, and then add the garlic and green onion mixture. Stir in the herbs and season with pepper to taste, mixing well.

Add the cheddar cheese and work the mixture together to for a stiff paste. Cover and chill until ready to serve.

To make the Melba toast, toast the slices of spelt bread on both sides, and then cut off the crusts.

Using a sharp bread knife, cut through the slices horizontally to make very thin slices.

Cut into triangles and then lightly grill the untoasted sides

Arrange the mixed salad leaves on 4 serving plates with the cherry tomatoes. Pile the cheese pâté on top and sprinkle with a little paprika.

Sweet Cinnamon Butter

Ingredients:
1 stick soft butter
1½ teaspoon cinnamon
15-18 drops stevia (sugar) (see glossary for definition)

Directions:
Blend together all three ingredients. Store in the refrigerator. Use on warm breads or pancakes.

Sun-Dried Tomato Pesto

Ingredients:

1 cup (8½ ounce jar) sun-dried tomatoes in oil, drained and chopped
2 tablespoons olive oil
6 fresh sage leaves
1 or 2 garlic cloves, to taste

Directions:

Put all of the ingredients in a blender or food processor and blend to a paste. Spread on spelt bread or any healthy organic crackers or breads.

Makes 1 cup

Breads

Banana Oat Bread

Ingredients:
2 cups oat flour
¼ teaspoon salt
¾ cup mashed banana
2 teaspoons baking powder
2 eggs
3 tablespoons cold water
2 tablespoons olive oil
½ cup chopped pecans or walnuts

Directions:
Grease 8x8 inch pan.

Mix dry ingredients.

Beat eggs. Add water, oil, and mashed bananas.

Blend with dry ingredients.

Add pecans or walnuts.

Bake 25-30 minutes in 350°F oven.

Makes 1 loaf

Cheesy Herb Spelt Bread

Ingredients:

2 cups spelt flour
2 teaspoons baking powder
1 teaspoon salt
1 teaspoon chicken stock (see recipe in soup section)
1 teaspoon dried rosemary
2 tablespoons fresh dill, chopped
2 tablespoons fresh chives, snipped
1 teaspoon dried sage
6 ounces grated cheddar cheese
1 egg, lightly beaten
5 fluid ounces skim milk
1 ounce butter, melted

Directions:

Place flour, baking powder, salt, chicken stock, rosemary, dill, chives, sage and 4 ounces of cheese in a bowl and mix to combine.

Combine egg, milk and butter. Add egg mixture to dry ingredients and mix to combine.

Spoon mixture into a greased and lined 11"x4½"x8½" loaf tin, sprinkle with remaining cheese and bake for 45 minutes or until cooked when tested with a toothpick. Turn onto a wire rack to cool.

Makes 1 loaf

Cinnamon-Raisin Bagels

Ingredients:

1 cup raisins
1½ cups lukewarm water
¼ cup xylitol (sugar) (see glossary for definition)
2 tablespoons honey
4 teaspoons active dry yeast
1 tablespoon canola oil
1¼ cups unbleached whole wheat flour
4 teaspoons ground cinnamon
1 tablespoon salt
3-4 cups spelt flour
1 large egg white, lightly beaten

Kettle Water:

6 quarts water
2 tablespoons xylitol

Directions:

Put raisins in a small bowl and add enough boiling water to cover; let stand for 5 minutes. Drain and blot dry with a paper towel.

Whisk lukewarm water, ¼ cup xylitol, honey, yeast and oil in a large bowl until the yeast dissolves. Stir in unbleached whole-wheat flour, cinnamon, salt and the raisins. Stir in enough of the spelt flour to make a soft dough, about 2½ cups.

Turn the dough out onto a lightly floured surface. Knead, gradually incorporating more spelt flour, until the dough is smooth and quite firm, 10 to 12 minutes. Cover with a clean cloth and let rest for 10 minutes.

Divide the dough into 12 pieces. Roll each piece into a 10 inch long rope. Form bagels by overlapping the ends by 1 inch. Pinch together firmly. Set the bagels aside, uncovered, to rise until slightly puffy, about 20 minutes.

To kettle and bake bagels: Preheat oven to 450°F. Line a large or 2 small baking sheets with parchment paper. In a large pot, bring 6 quarts of water and 2 tablespoons xylitol to a boil. Slip several risen bagels at a time into the pot. The water should be at a lively simmer. Cook for 45 seconds, turn them over with a slotted spoon and cook for 45 seconds longer. Remove the bagels with a slotted spoon and drain on a clean kitchen towel. Place on the prepared baking sheets. Brush with egg white.
Place the bagels in the oven, reduce heat to 425°F and bake for 15 minutes. Turn the bagels over and bake until golden brown, about 5 minutes more.

Makes 12 three ounce bagels

Croutons

Ingredients:
1 cup cubed unbleached whole-wheat bread or spelt bread (see recipe in this section)
2 teaspoons olive oil

Directions:
Preheat oven to 350°F. Toss cubed bread with oil. Spread onto a baking sheet and bake until golden brown, turning once during baking, 20 to 25 minutes.

Makes 4 servings, ¼ cup each

Raisin Bread

Ingredients:
1 box (15 ounces) raisins
1 cup apple juice
2 packages dry active yeast (¼ ounce each)
½ cup warm water
¾ cup plus 2 tablespoons butter
1 cup xylitol (sugar) (see glossary for definition)
1 teaspoon salt
2 teaspoons fresh lemon peel, grated
2 teaspoons almond extract
5 cups 2% milk
5 cups white spelt flour, sifted
5 cups whole-grain spelt flour
4 eggs, well beaten

Directions:
Place the raisins and apple juice in a bowl. Cover the bowl with plastic wrap. Soak at room temperature overnight. The following day, drain and discard the excess apple juice, reserving the raisins.

Place the yeast and warm water in a glass bowl. Stir and set aside for 5 to 10 minutes.

Place the butter, sugar, salt, lemon peel, and almond extract in a 3-4 quart bowl and cream together. Set aside.

Place the milk in a 2 quart saucepan, and cook over high heat just until bubbles form around the edges of the milk. DO NOT BOIL.

Pour the scaled milk over the reserved raisins. Add the raisin mixture to the butter mixture, and stir until the butter is completely melted.

Place the white spelt flour and the whole-grain spelt flour in a 4 quart bowl and mix well. When the butter mixture is cooled to lukewarm, add 2 cups of the flour mixture to the butter mixture, and beat with an electric mixer for about 2 minutes.

Add the yeast mixture to the dough and blend. Stir in half of the remaining flour, ½ cup at a time, until the dough is soft.

Turn the dough onto a lightly floured surface and knead for about 3 minutes, adding more flour if the dough is sticky. Grease a 5-6 quart bowl,

form the dough into a large smooth ball, and place in the bowl. Cover the bowl with a damp clean kitchen towel. Let the dough rise in a warm place for about 2 hours or until the dough is double in size.
Punch the dough down. Lift the dough out of the bowl, and set it aside. Grease the bowl again. Grease the ball of dough and return it to the bowl. Cover the dough with greased waxed paper and a towel.

Spray four 1 pound loaf pans with canola oil cooking spray. Lightly flour each pan. Divide the dough into 4 equal pieces. Form each piece into a loaf. Place each loaf into a pan, making sure that the ends of the pans are well filled to promote even rising. Cover the pans with clean kitchen towels and let dough rise in a warm place for about 2 hours, or until the loaves have doubled in size.

Preheat the oven to 375°F. Bake the loaves for 50 minutes, or until they sound hollow when tapped. Remove the loaves from the oven and cool slightly. Remove from the pans. Transfer the loaves to a wire rack and cool completely before serving or freezing.

Makes 4 1-pound loaves

Sweet Potato & Zucchini Bread

Ingredients:
2 cups spelt flour
2 teaspoons ground cinnamon
1 teaspoon baking soda
¼ teaspoon baking powder
¼ teaspoon salt
2 cups xylitol (sugar) (see glossary for definition)
¾ canola oil
3 large eggs
1 teaspoon vanilla extract
1½ cups zucchini, grated
1½ cups sweet potato, peeled and grated
1 cup walnuts, chopped

Directions:
Preheat oven to 350°F. Butter and spelt flour a 9"x5"x3" loaf pan. Sift the first five ingredients into a medium bowl. Beat xylitol, oil, eggs and vanilla to blend in a large bowl. Mix in zucchini and sweet potato. Add dry ingredients and walnuts and stir well.

Transfer batter to prepared pan. Bake until tester inserted into center comes out clean, about 1 hour 20 minutes. Cool bread in pan on rack for 15 minutes. Cut around the edge of the bread to loosen. Turn out onto rack and cool completely.

Makes 1 loaf

Spelt Bread

Ingredients:
3 cups warm water
1 tablespoon honey
2 tablespoons dry yeast
4 cups white spelt flour, sifted
3 cups white spelt flour

Directions:
In a large bowl, dissolve the honey and yeast in warm water and stir in 1 cup of the sifted flour. Set the bowl in a sink with very warm water until the liquid is bubbling, about 15 minutes.

Using an electric mixer, beat the remaining 3 cups of sifted flour on low speed. When the flour is moist, continue beating on medium speed for 3 minutes. Gradually stir the remaining 3 cups of spelt flour into the dough, using a large spoon. Turn the dough out on a spelt floured surface and knead for 10 minutes.

Grease a large bowl with butter. Place the dough in it and turn once to grease the top surface of the dough. Cover with a damp dish towel and put in a warm place to rise.

When the dough is double in size, punch it down and knead briefly in the bowl for about 2 minutes. Cover and return to a warm place for about 1 hour.

Knead on a lightly spelt floured surface. Divide the dough into 2 equal pieces. Spray two loaf pans with spray canola oil and flour. Shape the dough into 2 loaves. Place each loaf in the pans. Cover with a towel and put in a warm place to let the bread rise to the top of the pans.

Preheat the oven to 425°F. Remove the towel and place the bread in the oven. Bake for 15 minutes. Reduce the heat to 350°F and bake for 30 more minutes. Tap the tops to check if done. The sound should be hollow.

Remove the loaves from the pans and lay on their sides on wire racks to cool.

Makes 2 loaves

Whole-Grain Spelt Buns

Ingredients:

3½ cups warm water, divided
2 packages dry yeast (¼ ounce each)
3 eggs
½ teaspoon baking soda
1 teaspoon salt
⅓ cup milk
⅓ cup canola oil
⅓ cup honey
11 cups whole-grain spelt flour
Nonstick canola cooking spray

Directions:

Place ½ cup of the water in a bowl and sprinkle with the yeast. Stir and set aside for 5 to 10 minutes.

Combine the remaining 3 cups of water, the eggs, and the baking soda, salt, milk, canola oil, and honey in a larger bowl. Add 4 cups of the whole-grain spelt flour and mix thoroughly. Set aside for 15 minutes.

Add the yeast mixture to the flour mixture and mix thoroughly. Add enough of the remaining spelt flour to make a stiff dough.

Turn the dough onto a lightly spelt floured surface and knead for 10 minutes until the dough is smooth and elastic. Grease a large bowl with butter and place the dough in the bowl, turning over once to get the bottom and the top greased. Cover the bowl with a clean, damp kitchen towel and let rise in a warm place for 1 to 1½ hours or until the dough has doubled in size.

Punch down the dough and divide it into 20 equal-sized pieces. Arrange the pieces on the surface, spacing them 1 inch apart and allow the dough to sit for 10 minutes.

Lightly coat two cookie sheets with nonstick canola cooking spray. Using spelt floured hands, shape the dough into buns and place the buns on the prepared cookie sheets, spacing them about 2 inches apart. Cover the buns with a clean kitchen towel and let rise for 45 minutes to 1 hour, or until the buns have doubled in size.

Preheat the oven to 425°. Spray the buns lightly with the nonstick canola cooking spray and bake for about 15 minutes or until golden brown. Allow the buns to cool on the cookie sheets for 5-10 minutes. Transfer the buns to a wire rack, and cool completely before serving.

Makes 20 buns

Simple Spelt Yeast Bread

Ingredients:
1½ cups whole-grain spelt flour
2 packages dry yeast (¼ ounce each)
¼ teaspoon salt
1 cup plain yogurt
½ cup club soda
¼ cup honey
2 tablespoons butter
1 egg, beaten
1 cup whole-grain spelt flour

Directions:
Combine the 1½ cups of flour, the yeast, and the salt in a large bowl. Mix lightly and set aside.

Combine the yogurt, club soda, honey, and butter in a small saucepan. Place over medium heat and cook until the mixture is warm, but not too hot to touch with your fingers. DO NOT BOIL.

Add the yogurt mixture to the flour mixture, and stir to combine. Add the egg and mix the ingredients with an electric mixer or food processor set at a low speed until the dry ingredients are moistened. Increase to a medium speed and beat for 3 additional minutes. Add the remaining 1 cup of flour and mix thoroughly.

Coat a 1½ quart casserole dish with nonstick canola cooking spray. Pour the batter into the dish. Cover with a clean, damp kitchen towel and let rise in a warm place for 1 to 1½ hours, or until the dough has reached the top of the dish.

Preheat the oven to 375°F. Bake the loaf for 35 to 40 minutes or until golden brown in color and when tapped sounds hollow. Allow the bread to cool in the dish for 5 minutes. Remove the loaf from the dish and transfer to a wire rack. Serve warm.

Makes 1 round loaf

Whole Wheat or White Spelt Pizza Dough

Ingredients:
1½ cups whole-wheat **or** white spelt flour
1 package dry yeast
¾ teaspoon salt
¼ teaspoon xylitol (sugar) (see glossary for definition)
½-⅔ cup hot water (120-130°F)
2 teaspoons olive oil

Directions:
Combine whole-wheat spelt flour **or** white spelt flour, yeast, salt and xylitol in a blender or food processor. Mix well. Combine hot water and oil in a measuring cup. With the motor running, gradually pour in enough of the hot liquid until the mixture forms a sticky ball. The dough should be quite soft. If it seems dry, add 1 to 2 tablespoons warm water; if too sticky, add 1 to 2 tablespoons spelt flour. Blend or process until the dough forms a ball. Blend or process for another 1 minute to knead.

Transfer the dough to a lightly spelt floured surface. Coat a sheet of plastic wrap with canola cooking spray and place it, sprayed side down, over the dough. Let the dough rest for 10 to 20 minutes before rolling.

Makes 1-12 ounce pizza crust

Breakfast

Apple & Bran Muffins

Ingredients:
1½ cups whole-wheat flour
½ teaspoon ground nutmeg
1½ teaspoon baking powder
½ cup bran cereal, toasted
⅓ cup xylitol (sugar) (see glossary for definition)
2 green apples, grated
2 eggs, lightly beaten
¼ cup yogurt
1 tablespoon canola oil

Directions:
Sift together flour, nutmeg and baking powder into a bowl. Add bran cereal and xylitol and mix to combine.

Make a well in the center of flour mixture. Add apples, eggs, yogurt, and canola oil and mix until just combined.

Spoon mixture into twelve greased ½ cup muffin tins and bake for 15 minutes or until muffins are cooked when tested with a toothpick and toothpick is clean.

Makes 12 muffins

Applesauce Muffins

Ingredients:
¾ cup spelt flour
1½ tablespoon baking powder
1½ cups bran cereal
¾ cup unsweetened applesauce
2 eggs
½ cup xylitol (sugar) (see glossary for definition)
Dash salt
1 tablespoon cinnamon
½ teaspoon allspice
¾ cup milk

Directions:
Mix all ingredients above and put into 15 to 18 greased muffin tins.

Topping:
¼ cup xylitol (sugar) (see glossary for definition)
⅓ cup oatmeal ground for 15 seconds in blender

Directions:
Mix oatmeal and xylitol together and sprinkle on each muffin. Bake at 350°F for 20 to 25 minutes.

Makes 15 to 18 muffins

Banana-Walnut Oatmeal

Ingredients:
1 cup 1% milk
¾ cup water
pinch of salt
1 cup quick oats
1 very ripe banana, mashed
1 tablespoon maple syrup
1 tablespoon walnuts, chopped

Directions:
Combine milk, water and salt in a medium saucepan; heat until almost boiling.

Add oats and cook, stirring, until creamy, 1 to 2 minutes. Remove from the heat and stir in mashed banana and maple syrup.

Divide between 2 bowls, sprinkle with walnuts and serve.

Makes 2 servings, about 1 cup each

Blueberry Muffins

Ingredients:

2 cups Quaker Oat Bran Hot Cereal, uncooked
3 tablespoons xylitol (sugar) (see glossary for definition)
2 teaspoons baking powder
1 plain yogurt (8 ounces)
2 egg whites, slightly beaten
¼ cup 2% milk
¼ cup honey
2 tablespoons canola oil
1 teaspoon lemon peel, grated
½ cup fresh or frozen blueberries

Directions:

Preheat oven to 450°F. before mixing.

Mix together all ingredients and fold in blueberries.

Fill muffin cups almost full.

Bake 18 to 20 minutes or until golden brown and toothpick comes out clean when stuck into muffin.

Makes 12 muffins

Breakfast Pizza

Ingredients:

1 tablespoon olive oil
½ teaspoon salt
½ cup onions, chopped
½ cup green pepper, chopped
1 clove garlic, minced
1 teaspoon sage
½ teaspoon parsley
8 eggs
8 slices cheddar cheese or 1 cup cheddar cheese, grated
1 cup mozzarella cheese, grated

Directions:

Make pizza crust according to directions (see recipe in bread section). Bake crust at 350°F for 10 minutes. When crust comes out of the oven, layer cheddar cheese on top of crust.

Sauté vegetables and spices in oil.

In a separate bowl beat eggs until yolks and whites are blended. Pour over vegetables and cook over medium heat, stirring constantly until moist, but cooked.

Spread mixture over crust and cheese. Top with mozzarella cheese and bake at 350°F for 10 minutes or until cheese is melted.

Makes 6 to 8 servings

Cottage Cheese Crêpes with Cherries

Ingredients:

Crêpes

⅓ cup kamut flour
2 tablespoons whole wheat flour
⅛ teaspoon salt
⅓ cup apple juice
½ cup plus 1-2 tablespoons water
1 large egg, lightly beaten
4 teaspoons butter

Filling

1 cup cottage cheese or ricotta cheese, at room temperature
2 cups sweet cherries, pitted
¼ cup maple syrup

Directions:

Crêpes

In a large bowl, combine the kamut flour, whole wheat flour, and salt.

In a small bowl, whisk together the apple juice, ½ cup water, egg, and 2 teaspoons of butter. Whisk into the flour mixture to make a smooth batter.

Melt 1 teaspoon of the remaining butter in an 8" nonstick skillet coated with canola oil cooking spray over medium heat. Pour 3 tablespoons of batter into the skillet and tilt the skillet to coat the bottom with a thin layer of the batter. (If the batter seems too thick, add 1 to 2 tablespoons water.) Cook the first side for 1 minute, or until lightly browned. Turn and cook the second side for 30 to 60 seconds.

Slide the crepe onto a plate. Cover with foil to keep warm.

Continue making crêpes in the same fashion; add in the last teaspoon of butter to the pan after making the second crêpe.

Filling

Place a crêpe on a plate, attractive side down.

Arrange ¼ cup of the cheese and ½ cup of the cherries in a line in the center of the crêpe and fold in quarters. Repeat with the remaining ingredients to make 4 crêpes.

Drizzle with syrup.

Makes 4 crêpes

Cottage Cheese Parfaits

Ingredients:
1 cup unsweetened applesauce
2 cups cottage cheese
1 can mandarin orange slices packed in juice (11 ounce), drained
¼ teaspoon ground nutmeg

Directions:
Layer ¼ of each of the first three ingredients in the listed order in a parfait glass.

Repeat with the three additional glasses.

Top each parfait with a pinch of nutmeg

Makes 4 parfaits

Lemon-Poppy Seed Muffins

Ingredients:
Muffins
2 eggs, lightly beaten
1 cup sour cream (8 ounces)
½ cup 2% milk
¼ cup canola oil
¼ cup honey
3 tablespoons poppy seeds
1 tablespoon lemon rind, grated
2¼ cups spelt flour, sifted
3 teaspoons baking powder

Lemon cream-cheese icing
2 ounces cream cheese, softened
1 tablespoon lemon juice
¾ cup xylitol (sugar) (see glossary for definition)

Directions:
Muffins
Place eggs, sour cream, milk, canola oil, honey, poppy seeds and lemon rind in a bowl and mix well to combine.

Add spelt flour and baking powder to poppy seed mixture and mix until just combined.

Spoon mixture in six canola oil sprayed muffin tins.

Bake for 25 to 30 minutes or until muffins are cooked when tested with a toothpick and the toothpick comes out clean after being stuck into the muffin.

Icing
To make icing, place cream cheese, lemon juice, and xylitol in a bowl and beat with a mixer until smooth. Top cold muffins with icing. (Because you are using xylitol, icing will not be white as when using powdered sugar. It will just appear as a glaze.)

Makes 6 muffins

Sausage and Cheese Breakfast Muffins

Ingredients:

4 ounces turkey sausage or crumbled turkey bacon
½ green bell pepper, chopped
¼ onion, chopped
5 large eggs
1 can (12 ounces) sliced mushrooms, drained
½ cup (2 ounces) shredded cheddar cheese

Directions

Preheat the oven to 350°F. Coat a 6 cup nonstick muffin pan with canola cooking spray.

In a medium nonstick skillet over medium-high heat, cook the sausage, pepper and onion for 5 minutes, or until the sausage is no longer pink. Spoon the mixture into a bowl and cool slightly. Stir in the eggs and mushrooms. Evenly divide the mixture among the prepared muffin cups. Sprinkle with cheese.

Bake for 20 minutes, or until the egg is set.

Makes 6 muffins

Sesame-Seed Flapjacks

Ingredients:

1 package yeast
1 cup warm water
1 cup whole-grain spelt flour
2 tablespoons molasses
⅓ cup ground sesame seeds
¼ cup 2% milk
dash of salt
3 tablespoons canola oil

Directions:

Place the yeast and water in a small bowl and allow to stand for 5 minutes at room temperature.

Place all the remaining ingredients except the oil in a 2-3 quart bowl and mix.

Pour the yeast mixture into the flour mixture and mix well.

Grease a skillet with 1 tablespoon of the canola oil, and heat it over medium-high heat. When the oil is hot but not smoking, reduce the heat to medium. Drop the batter onto the pan, using 2 tablespoons for each flapjack. Make sure the flapjacks do not run into each other. When bubbles form on the surface of the flapjacks, turn them over with a spatula and brown on the other side.

Remove the cooked flapjacks from the pan and keep them warm in the oven until all the flapjacks are cooked. Before starting each new batch, add oil as necessary and allow it to heat before spooning in more batter.

Serve hot with a topping of your choice.

Makes 20 pancakes

Spinach Breakfast Casserole

Ingredients:
4 slices toasted spelt bread, cut into ½" cubes. (see recipe in bread section)
2 cups spinach leaves, washed and finely chopped
¾ cup monterey jack cheese, grated
¾ cup cheddar cheese, grated
6 eggs
2 cups 2% milk
½ teaspoon dry mustard
salt and pepper to taste

Directions:
Generously spray a 9 x 13 inch glass casserole pan with canola cooking spray. Arrange the bread cubes over the bottom of the dish. Spread the spinach over the bread, and sprinkle with the cheeses.

Place the eggs, milk, and spices in a large bowl. Beat thoroughly with a wire whisk. Pour the egg mixture over the casserole dish mixture. Cover the dish with aluminum foil and refrigerate overnight.

Preheat the oven to 350°F. Remove the cover from the dish and bake for 45 minutes or just until the egg mixture is firm. Serve hot.

Makes 6 servings

Swiss & Fennel Quiche

Ingredients: Crust
1¼ cups whole wheat spelt flour
¼ teaspoon salt
2 tablespoons canola oil
2 tablespoons butter, cold and cut into small pieces
2-3 tablespoons ice water

Ingredients: Filling
1 cup fennel bulb, thinly sliced
6 medium scallions, chopped
4 eggs
1 cup evaporated milk
½ cup skim milk
1½ teaspoons Dijon mustard
¼ teaspoon ground nutmeg
¼ teaspoon ground black pepper
½ cup (2 ounces) shredded swiss cheese
1 tablespoon grated parmesan cheese
pinch of paprika

Directions: Crust
Preheat the oven to 425°F. Spray a 9" pie plate with canola cooking spray.

In a large bowl, blender or food processor, combine the flour and salt. Blend briefly to mix. Add the oil and butter and blend until the mixture resembles fine meal. While stirring constantly with the food processor or blender running, add the water, 1 tablespoon at a time, and stir or process for 30 seconds, or until the dough barely comes together. Remove to a spelt floured surface and pat the dough into a flattened disk.

Place the dough between 2 sheets of waxed paper and roll out to an 11" circle. Remove the top sheet and invert the dough into the prepared pie plate. Remove the remaining sheet of waxed paper and fit the dough into the plate. Use a fork to poke holes in the bottom and sides of the dough.

Bake for 10 minutes. Check to make sure that dough is not getting air under it and bake for 4 minutes longer or until the dough is dry but has not begun to brown.

Directions: Filling
Heat a medium nonstick frying pan coated with canola cooking spray over medium heat. Add the fennel bulb and cook for 5 minutes, or until soft. Add the scallions and cook for 2 minutes.

In a medium bowl, whisk together the eggs, evaporated milk, skim milk, mustard, nutmeg, and pepper.

Sprinkle the fennel mixture over the bottom of the baked pie shell and top with the swiss cheese. Pour in the egg mixture and sprinkle the top with the parmesan cheese and paprika.

Bake for 30 minutes or until a knife inserted in the center comes out clean. Cool on a rack for 10 minutes.

Makes 6 servings

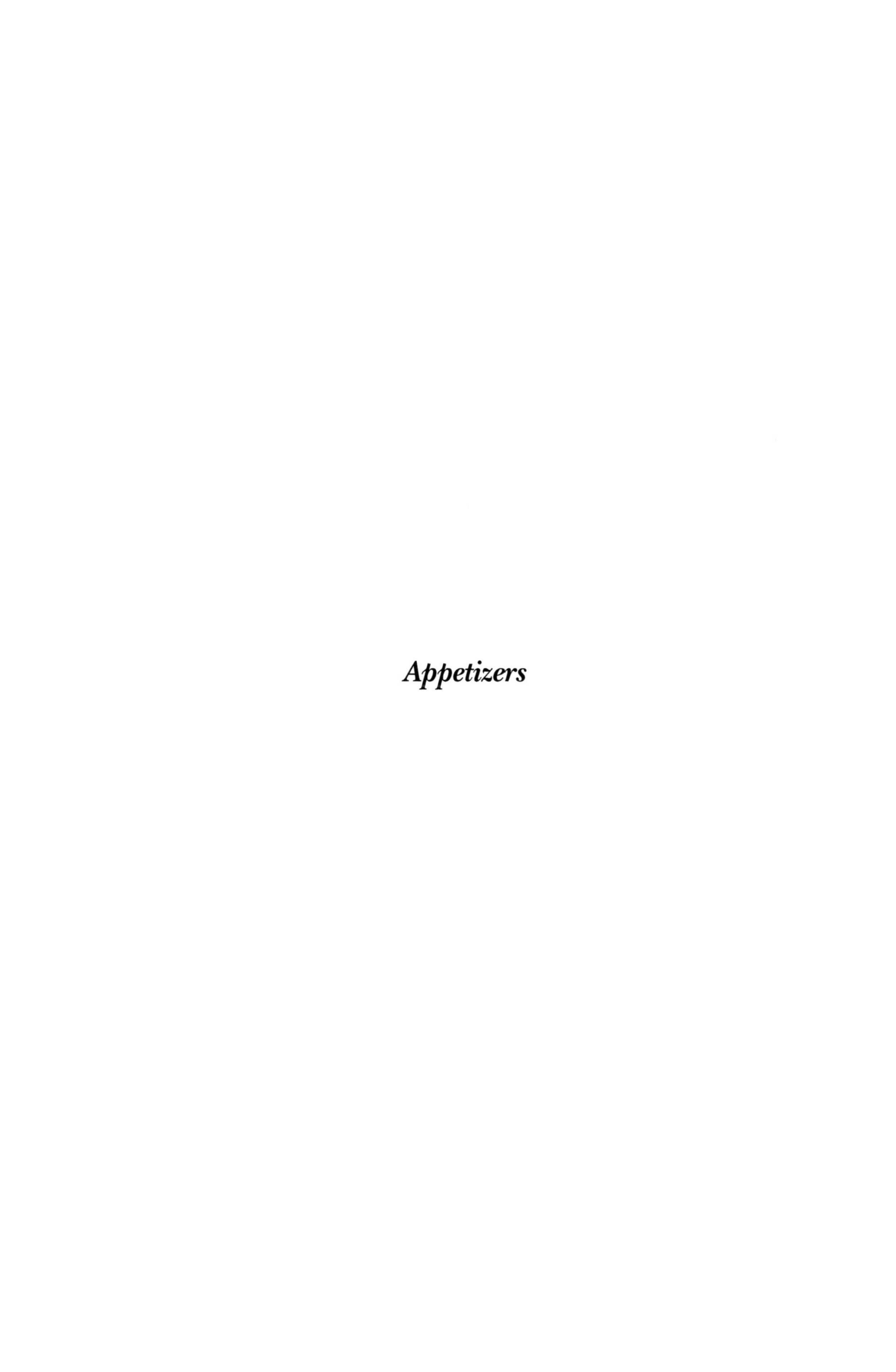

Appetizers

Mini-Calzones

Ingredients:
Spelt Dough (recipe follows)
2 tablespoons olive oil
2 tablespoons minced onion
4 cups coarsely chopped, lightly packed spinach
¼ cup part skim ricotta cheese
½ teaspoon ground nutmeg

Directions:
Prepare Spelt Flour Dough (see below). While the dough is rising, prepare filling. Heat 1 tablespoon of the oil in a wide frying pan over medium heat. Add onions; cook, stirring occasionally, until onion is soft (about 5 minutes). Add spinach and cook, stirring often, until liquid has evaporated (about 5 minutes). Remove from heat. Add ricotta cheese and nutmeg; mix well. Let cool.

Punch Spelt Flour Dough down and knead briefly on a lightly floured board to release air. Shape dough into a ball, then roll out ⅛ inch thick. Cut dough into 3-inch rounds. Place about 1 teaspoon of the spinach filling on half of each round. Fold plain half of each round over filling; press edges together and seal. Transfer calzones to oiled, cornmeal-dusted baking sheets. Brush tops with remaining 1 tablespoon olive oil; prick tops with a fork.

Bake calzones in a 425° oven until lightly browned (about 15 minutes). Serve warm. If made ahead, let cool, then cover and refrigerate for up to 1 day. To reheat, arrange on baking sheets and heat, uncovered, in a 425° oven for about 5 minutes.

SPELT FLOUR DOUGH
In a large bowl, combine 1 package active dry yeast and ¾ cup warm water (about 110°); let stand until yeast is softened (about 5 minutes). Add 1 teaspoon each salt and 1 teaspoon of xylitol (sugar) (see glossary for definition); stir in 1 cup spelt flour (see glossary for definition) Beat with a heavy spoon or an electric mixer until smooth. Then mix in about 1 cup more of spelt flour or enough to make dough hold together. Turn dough out onto a lightly floured board and knead until smooth and elastic (about 5 minutes), adding more spelt flour as needed to prevent sticking. Place dough in an olive oiled bowl and turn over to oil the top; cover with plastic wrap and let rise in a warm place until almost double in size (about 1 hour).

Makes about 36 calzones

Egg-Dipped Cauliflower or Broccoli

Ingredients:
3 cups bite-size cauliflower
3 cups bite-size broccoli
2 eggs, beaten
Olive oil for frying
salt to taste
Parmesan cheese to taste

Directions:
Combine the cauliflower florets and broccoli florets in a large, deep saucepan or 1½ quart casserole dish with about 1 inch of water. Steam over medium heat or microwave for about 2 minutes, at which time it should be quite underdone and then drain.

Stir the cauliflower and broccoli pieces into the beaten egg until evenly coated.

Heat just enough oil to coat the bottom of a wide skillet. When hot, arrange some of the cauliflower pieces and broccoli pieces in a single layer (you will need to cook them in 2 or 3 batches). Cook over medium heat, turning frequently until the pieces are golden and crisp. Season with salt and/or parmesan cheese. Keep each batch warm in a covered container while preparing the next and serve.

Makes four to six servings

Cottage Cheese-Stuffed Celery

Ingredients:
½ cup reduced-fat cottage cheese
1 small onion, chopped
⅛ teaspoon prepared horseradish
⅛ teaspoon Worcestershire sauce
Pinch of garlic powder
4 ribs celery, cut into 3" pieces
Paprika, to garnish

Directions:
In a small bowl, combine the cottage cheese, onion, horseradish, Worcestershire sauce, and garlic; mix thoroughly. Spoon into the celery pieces. Sprinkle with paprika to garnish.

Makes 4 servings

Hot Cheese Puffs

Ingredients:
1 cup shredded cheddar cheese
3 teaspoons soft butter
½ cup spelt flour (see glossary for definition)
1 teaspoon paprika
½ teaspoon Worcestershire sauce
Dash cayenne pepper
Salt to taste
24 medium stuffed olives

Directions:
Preheat oven to 400°. Cream cheese and butter, blend in rest. Mold 1 teaspoon dough around each olive covering completely. Place on ungreased cookie sheet. Bake at 400° for 12 minutes or until golden brown.

Makes 24 puffs

Apricot-Orange Glazed Chicken

Ingredients:
thirty-six 6-to 8-inch bamboo skewers
6 boneless, skinless chicken breast halves (approximately 2 lbs of chicken)
1 cup unsweetened apricot jam
1½ tablespoon Stevia (sugar) (see glossary for definition)
2 tablespoons prepared horseradish
2 tablespoons minced ginger
2 tablespoons finely grated orange peel
2 tablespoons brown sugar
¼ cups unsweetened orange juice

Directions:
Soak thirty-six 6 - to 8-inch bamboo skewers in hot water to cover for at least 30 minutes.

Rinse chicken and pat dry. Cut each chicken breast half lengthwise into 6 equal slices, then weave each slice onto a skewer. Place skewers on a lightly canola oiled rack in a broiler pan.

In a 1- to 1½-quart pan, combine jam, horseradish, ginger, orange peel, brown sugar, and unsweetened orange juice. Stir over medium-high heat until jam is melted; keep mixture warm.

Brush chicken with some of the jam mixture. Broil 6 inches below heat, turning once and brushing 2 or 3 times with remaining jam mixture, until meat in thickest part is no longer pink; cut to test (about 8 minutes). Brush with any remaining jam mixture; serve hot.

Makes 36 appetizers

Granola Mix

Ingredients:

1 carton (18 oz) old-fashioned oatmeal (approximately 6 cups)
⅔ cup honey
⅓ cup packed light-brown sugar
¼ cup canola oil
1 tablespoon vanilla extract
1 teaspoon ground cinnamon
1 cup slivered almonds
1 cup shelled sunflower seeds
Optional: dried apricots and sweetened dried cranberries for mixing with granola just before using.

Directions:

Heat oven to 325°F. Have ready 2 rimmed baking sheets. Spread oatmeal evenly on both baking sheets. Bake 12 to 15 minutes, stirring occasionally, until slightly toasted.

Meanwhile whisk honey, brown sugar, canola oil, vanilla and cinnamon in a large bowl until well blended. Add toasted oats, nuts and seeds; stir until thoroughly coated. Spread evenly on both baking sheets and, stirring occasionally, bake 20 to 30 minutes until evenly toasted. Cool completely on sheets on a wire rack.

Scrape from pan to break up. Store airtight with fruit packed separately and added when snack is going to be eaten. Store at room temperature for up to one month or in the refrigerator for up to two months.

Makes 10 cups

Cheesy Popcorn

Ingredients:
1 package of unbuttered microwave popcorn
1 tablespoon extra-virgin olive oil or canola oil
Pinch of cayenne pepper (can be eliminated if not desired)
¼ cup parmesan cheese

Directions:
Microwave one bag of popcorn according to the directions on the bag. Transfer popcorn from the original bag to a large zip lock or plastic bag and add olive oil and parmesan cheese to the popcorn. Shake until popcorn is thoroughly covered with coating of cheese mixture.

Makes four servings (approximately)

Potato Skins with Chicken & Almond Topping

Ingredients:
4 baking potatoes
¼ cup of melted butter
1 can cooked chicken
¼ cup pine nuts
¼ cup finely chopped onion
8 teaspoons sour cream
¼ teaspoon black pepper

Directions:
Preheat the oven to 350°F. Wash and dry four baking potatoes. Pierce each potato with a fork and place potatoes in the preheated oven. Bake for 30 minutes or until the center is firm but can be easily pierced with a fork.

Cool the potatoes, cut each potato in quarters lengthwise. Cut the center of the potato out of each quarter leaving the skin with about ½" of potato on it.

Brush the skins with melted butter, then sprinkle them with salt and pepper. Bake them at 350°F for 10 minutes.

Mix potato pulp taken out of the four potatoes, can of cooked chicken, pine nuts, chopped onion, and sour cream.

Fill each potato skin quarter with topping. Bake for another 5 -10 minutes until warmed.

Makes 16 potato skins

Roasted Potatoes Parmesan

Ingredients:
16 small red thin-skinned potatoes, scrubbed
⅓ cup grated parmesan cheese
⅓ cup plain yogurt
2 tablespoons minced onion
Paprika

Directions:
Pierce each potato in several places with a fork. Arrange in a single layer in a shallow baking pan. Bake in a 375° oven until tender when pierced (about 1 hour). Let cool slightly. (At this point, you may cover and refrigerate up to a day)

In a small bowl, mix cheese, yogurt, and onion.

To fill potatoes, cut each in half. Scoop out a small depression from center of cut side of each potato half. Set halves, cut sides up in a shallow rimmed baking pan. Spoon cheese mixture into potato halves. Sprinkle generously with paprika. Bake in a 350° oven until heated through (about 15 minutes). Serve hot.

Makes 32 appetizers

Soft Pretzels

Ingredients:
2 cups warm water
1 package active dry yeast
1 teaspoon xylitol (sugar) (see glossary for definition)
1 teaspoon salt
4 cups (approx.) spelt flour (see glossary for definition)
2 tablespoons baking soda
1 tablespoons kosher or coarse sea salt

Directions:
In large bowl, combine 1½ cups warm water, yeast, and xylitol (sugar); stir to dissolve. Let stand until foamy, about 5 minutes. Add salt and 2 cups spelt flour; beat well with wooden spoon. Gradually stir in 1½ cups flour to make soft dough.

Turn dough onto floured surface and knead until smooth and elastic, about 6 minutes, kneading in enough of remaining ½ cup flour just to keep dough from sticking.

Shape dough into ball; place in greased large bowl, turning dough to grease top. Cover bowl with plastic wrap and let dough rise in warm place (80° to 85°F) until doubled in volume, about 30 minutes.

Preheat oven to 400°F. Grease two cookie sheets with butter. Punch down dough and cut into 12 equal pieces. Roll each piece into 24-inch long rope. Shape ropes into loop-shaped pretzels.

In a small bowl, whisk remaining ½ cup warm water and baking soda until soda has dissolved.

Dip pretzels in baking-soda mixture and place 1½ inches apart on prepared cookie sheets; sprinkle with kosher or coarse sea salt. Bake until browned, 16 to 18 minutes, rotating cookie sheets between upper and lower oven racks halfway through baking. Serve pretzels warm, or transfer to wire racks to cool.

Makes 12 pretzels

Soups

Chicken Stock

Ingredients:
8 cups water
3 pounds skinless chicken parts, including bones
2 cups chopped carrot greens
2 cups chopped celery stalks and leaves
2 large onions, chopped
1 turnip, peeled and grated
1 clove garlic, minced
4 whole peppercorns
½ cup chopped fresh parsley and thyme
½-inch piece fresh ginger (optional)

Directions:
Combine all ingredients in a 5-quart kettle, and bring to a boil over high heat. Reduce the heat to medium-low, cover, and simmer for 3 hours

Remove and discard the chicken pieces and vegetables, and cool the stock to room temperature. Place the covered pot in the refrigerator, and chill for 4 hours, or until the fat congeals on the surface of the soup. Skim off and discard the fat.

Place the pot over high heat, and cook the stock nearly to the boiling point. Remove the pot from the heat, and strain the stock by pouring it through a large strainer. Transfer the stock to containers with tight-fitting lids or to ice cube trays, and refrigerate or freeze until needed.

Makes 2 quarts

Vegetable Stock

Ingredients:
8 cups water
4 cups diced, unpeeled, well-scrubbed potatoes and turnips
2 cups chopped carrot greens
2 cups chopped celery stalks and leaves
2 large onions, chopped
4-5 scallion tops, chopped
1 clove garlic, minced
4 whole peppercorns
1 bay leaf
½ cup chopped fresh garden herbs such as parsley, dill and basil

Directions:
Combine all of the ingredients in a 5 quart kettle, and bring to a boil over high heat. Reduce the heat to medium-low, cover and simmer for 2 hours.

Remove the pot from the heat, and strain the stock by pouring it through a large strainer. Discard the solids. Transfer the stock to containers with tight lids or to ice cube trays, and refrigerate or freeze until needed.

Makes 2 quarts

Spelt Flour and Cheese Soup

Ingredients:
¼ cup butter
½ cup spelt flour (see glossary for definition)
5 cups water, vegetable stock or chicken stock (find recipe for stocks at beginning of soup section)
½ teaspoon dried basil, or 1 teaspoon chopped fresh basil
salt to taste
Freshly ground white pepper to taste
¼ cup grated parmesan cheese

Directions:
Place the butter in a 2-quart saucepan, and melt over medium heat. Add the flour, and cook, stirring constantly with a spoon for about 3 minutes, or until the flour browns.

Add the water or stock to the saucepan, and beat the mixture with a wire whisk until smooth. Reduce the heat to low, and add the basil, salt, and pepper. Allow the mixture to simmer uncovered for 30 minutes, stirring occasionally. DO NOT BOIL.

Remove the pot from the heat, and stir the grated cheese into the soup. Transfer the soup to bowls, and serve immediately.

Makes 4 servings

Chicken Noodle Soup with Dill

Ingredients:
10 cups homemade chicken broth (see recipe at beginning of soup section above)
3 medium carrots, peeled and diced
1 large stalk celery, diced
3 tablespoons minced fresh ginger
6 cloves garlic, minced
4 ounces spelt noodles (3 cups)
4 cups shredded cooked skinless chicken (about 1 pound)
3 tablespoons chopped fresh dill
1 tablespoon lemon juice, or to taste

Directions:
Bring broth to a boil in a Dutch oven. Add carrots, celery, ginger and garlic; cook, uncovered, over medium heat until vegetables are just tender, approximately 20 minutes.

Add noodles and chicken; continue cooking until the noodles are just tender, 8-10 minutes. Stir in dill and lemon juice.

Makes 9 servings (approximately 1 cup each)

Minestrone Soup

Ingredients:
10 oz. dried white beans
6 cups water
6 cups homemade chicken stock (recipe found above at beginning of soup section)
4 oz. mushrooms, sliced
5 oz. green beans, chopped
2 carrots, chopped
2 zucchini, sliced
1 onion, sliced
5 oz. small spelt pasta shells
14 oz. canned tomatoes, undrained and mashed
freshly ground black pepper
grated parmesan cheese

Directions:
Place dried beans and 4 cups water in a large bowl, cover and set aside to soak for 8 hours or overnight.

Drain beans and rinse in cold water. Place beans and homemade stock in a large saucepan, bring to a boil and continue to boil for 10 minutes, then reduce heat, cover and simmer for 1 hour or until beans are tender.

Add mushrooms, green beans, carrots, zucchini, onion and remaining water to pan. Bring to a boil, then reduce heat, cover and simmer for 30 minutes.

Stir in spelt pasta and tomatoes and cook for 10 minutes longer or until pasta is tender. Season to taste with black pepper. Sprinkle with parmesan cheese and serve immediately.

Makes approximately 6 servings

Split Pea Soup

Ingredients:
2 teaspoons extra-virgin olive oil
2 carrots, diced
1 onion, chopped
1 potato, peeled and diced
1 sweet potato, peeled and diced
2 cloves garlic, minced
6 cups homemade chicken or vegetable stock (see recipes at beginning of soup section)
1 cup green split peas, rinsed
Freshly ground pepper to taste
4 slices turkey bacon, diced (optional)

Directions:
Heat oil in a Dutch oven or large pot over medium-high heat. Add carrots, onion, potato, sweet potato and garlic; cook, stirring, until softened, about 3 minutes. Add homemade stock and split peas and bring to a boil. Reduce heat to low and simmer, partially covered, until the vegetables are tender and the split peas have broken down, about 40 minutes. Season with pepper.

If using turkey bacon, cook in a small skillet over medium heat, stirring, until crisp, 3 to 5 minutes. Drain on paper towels.

Ladle the soup into bowls and garnish with bacon.

Makes approximately 6 servings, generous 1 cup each

Potato, Cauliflower & Watercress Soup

Ingredients:

1½ cups cauliflower flowerets, cut into bite-size pieces
2½ cups nonfat milk
2 tablespoons butter
½ cup minced onion
⅛ teaspoon ground nutmeg
2 large potatoes, pealed and diced
1¾ cups homemade chicken stock (see recipe at beginning of soup section)
8 cups lightly packed watercress sprigs
Salt and ground pepper
¼ to ⅓ cup plain yogurt or sour cream

Directions:

In a 2 to 3 quart pan, combine cauliflower and milk. Bring to a boil over medium heat; then reduce heat to medium-low and cook until cauliflower is tender when pierced (approximately 8-10 minutes). Place a strainer over a large bowl and pour cauliflower mixture through it; then set cauliflower and milk aside.

Rinse pan; set over medium heat and add butter. When butter is melted, add chopped onion and nutmeg; cook, stirring occasionally, until onion is soft but not browned (approximately 3 to 5 minutes). Add potatoes and homemade stock; increase heat to medium-high and bring to a boil. Reduce heat, cover, and simmer until potatoes are very tender when pierced (approximately 15 to 20 minutes). Reserve several watercress sprigs for garnish, then stir remaining watercress into potato mixture and cook, uncovered, for 5 minutes. Add cauliflower to pan and cook until heated through (approximately 3 minutes).

In a food processor or blender, whirl potato mixture, a portion at a time, until smooth. Return to pan, add reserved strained milk, and heat just until steaming (DO NOT BOIL). Season to taste with salt and pepper.

To serve, ladle soup into bowls. Garnish each serving with a spoonful of yogurt or sour cream and a watercress sprig.

Makes approximately 4 to 6 servings

Spiced Cream of Pumpkin Soup

Ingredients:
3 large leeks
1 tablespoon olive oil
½ cup currants
½ pound carrots, thinly sliced
3 cups homemade chicken stock (see recipe at beginning of soups section)
2 cups nonfat milk
1 can (1 lb.) solid-pack pumpkin
¼ teaspoon ground nutmeg
toasted pumpkin seeds (optional)

Directions:
Trim ends and all but 3 inches of green tops from leeks; remove tough outer leaves. Split leeks lengthwise; rinse well, then thinly slice crosswise. Set aside.

Heat oil in a 3 to 4 quart pan over medium heat; add currants and stir until puffed (about 2 minutes). Lift from pan with a slotted spoon; set aside. Add leeks and carrots to pan; stir often until leeks are golden (approximately 10 minutes). Add 1 cup of the homemade stock, bring to a boil, then reduce heat, cover and simmer until carrots are very tender to bite (approximately 10 minutes).

In a blender or food processor, whirl leek mixture until smooth. Return to pan and add remaining 2 cups homemade stock, milk, pumpkin, and nutmeg. Cook over medium heat, stirring often, until soup is hot (approximately 15 minutes). Stir in currants. Add pumpkin seeds to add to taste (optional).

Makes approximately 6 servings

Harvest Turkey Soup

Ingredients:
Canola oil cooking spray
1 pound ground skinless turkey
1 medium-size onion, chopped
1 teaspoon dry oregano
1 teaspoon Italian herb seasoning
3 large firm–ripe tomatoes, chopped
3 large carrots, thinly sliced
1 large potato, peeled and diced
6 cups homemade vegetable stock (see recipe at beginning of soup section)
2 cups tomato juice
1 tablespoon Worcestershire sauce
½ cup dry tiny spelt bow tie pasta or other small pasta shape
2 medium-size zucchini, coarsely diced
Liquid hot pepper seasoning (optional)

Directions:
Coat a wide 4 to 5 quart pan with cooking spray. Crumble turkey into pan; add onion, oregano, and herb seasoning. Cook over medium heat, stirring often, until turkey is no longer pink and onion is soft but not browned (approximately 5 minutes). Stir in tomatoes, carrots, potato, stock, tomato juice, and Worcestershire sauce. Increase heat to medium-high and bring to a boil; then reduce heat, cover, and boil gently for 20 minutes.

Add spelt pasta; cover and cook for 5 minutes. Stir in zucchini and boil gently, uncovered, until pasta and zucchini are just tender to bite (approximately 8 to 10 minutes). Season to taste with hot pepper seasoning (optional).

Makes approximately 6 to 8 servings

Roasted Vegetable & Cheese Soup

Ingredients:
2 medium size leeks
1 large ear corn, husk and silk removed
1 small red onion, cut in half
1 large red bell pepper
1 large yellow or green bell pepper
2 cloves garlic, peeled
4 cups homemade chicken stock (see recipe at beginning of soup section)
1 cup shredded sharp Cheddar cheese
½ cup sour cream

Directions:
Trim and discard roots and tough tops from leeks; remove and discard coarse outer leaves. Split leeks lengthwise; thoroughly rinse leek halves between layers. In a large, shallow baking pan, arrange leeks, corn, onion halves, and whole bell peppers.

Broil 4 to 6 inches below heat, turning vegetables as needed to brown evenly, for 10 minutes. Add garlic. Continue to broil, turning as needed, until vegetables are well charred (approximately 5 more minutes); remove vegetables from pan as they are charred. Cover vegetables loosely with foil and let stand until cool enough to handle (approximately 10 minutes).

With a sharp knife, cut corn kernels from cob. Remove and discard skins, seeds, and stems from bell peppers. Coarsely chop peppers, leeks, onion, and garlic.

In a 4 to 5 quart pan, combine vegetables and stock. Bring to a boil over high heat; then reduce heat, cover, and simmer for 10 minutes to blend flavors. Ladle soup into individual bowls; sprinkle with cheese, top with sour cream, and serve.

Makes approximately 4 servings

Salads

Apple Strawberry & Pecan Salad

Ingredients:
2 red apples, chopped
2 stalks celery, sliced
6 oz strawberries, halved
1 drop of stevia or 3 Tsp xylitol (sugar) (see glossary for definition of each)
2 oz chopped pecans

Dressing Ingredients:
2 teaspoons finely chopped fresh mint leaves
3 tablespoons vanilla yogurt
2 tablespoons lemon juice

Directions:
Combine apples, celery, strawberries, stevia **or** xylitol and pecans in a bowl

To make dressing, blend together mint, yogurt and lemon juice. Toss with apple mixture and refrigerate until required.

Note: A variation on the traditional Waldorf salad with half the fat and no cholesterol

Makes approximately 4 servings

Three Bean Salad

Ingredients:
1 can pinto beans
1 can red beans
1 can green beans
1 garlic clove, minced
1 small onion, minced
½ cup balsamic vinegar
¼ cup canola oil
15 drops stevia (sugar) (see glossary for definition)

Directions:
Stir vegetables together. Mix oil, stevia, and vinegar until well mixed. Pour over vegetables and chill.

Makes approximately 6-8 servings

Berry Delicious Salad

Ingredients:
SALAD
6 cups mixed salad greens
1 cup sliced fresh strawberries
¼ cup crumbled feta cheese or blue cheese
¼ cup chopped toasted pecans

DRESSING
2 tablespoons canola oil
¼ cup sliced fresh strawberries
1½ tablespoons raspberry or red wine vinegar
1½ teaspoon xylitol or honey
¼ teaspoon dried thyme
¼ teaspoon salt
⅛ teaspoon ground black pepper

Directions:
To make the salad: Place ¼ of the salad greens on each of four salad plates. Top the greens with ¼ of the berries, cheese, and pecans.

To make the dressing: Put all of the ingredients in a mini blender jar, and blend until smooth. Chill until ready to serve.

Drizzle a tablespoon of the dressing over each salad, and serve immediately

Makes 4 servings

Broccoli Salad

Ingredients:

3 cups broccoli tops
1 cup carrots, diced
1 celery stick, minced
1 green pepper, chopped
3 hard boiled eggs, chopped
2 tablespoons onion, chopped
¾ cup mayonnaise (see mayonnaise recipe in condiment section)
2 tablespoons balsamic vinegar
¼ cup water

Directions:

Steam broccoli and carrots until tender but still crisp. Drain and rinse in cool water. Mix mayonnaise, vinegar, and water until blended. Pour mixture over vegetables and mix well. Chill in refrigerator before serving.

Makes approximately 4-6 servings

Overnight Slaw

Ingredients:

¼-½ cup xylitol or 1 drop stevia (sugar) (see glossary for definition of each)
¼ cup lemon juice
¼ cup white vinegar
1 teaspoon celery salt
1 teaspoon garlic salt
1 small head cabbage, shredded
3 single stalks celery, chopped
½ green bell pepper, chopped
¼ cup fresh chives, chopped
¼ cup fresh radishes, sliced

Directions:

In a large bowl, whisk together the xylitol **or** stevia, lemon juice, vinegar, celery salt, and garlic salt. Add the cabbage, celery, green pepper, and chives and toss lightly. Cover and refrigerate overnight. Add the radishes immediately before serving.

Makes 4 servings

Zesty Cucumber Salad

Ingredients:
4 cucumbers
6 tablespoons vinegar
¼ cup onions, chopped
1 small clove of garlic
2 tablespoons chopped chives
2 tablespoons water
¼ teaspoon black pepper
3½ tablespoons dill weed
5 drops of stevia **or** ¼ cup xylitol (sugar) (see glossary for definition of each)

Directions:
Peel cucumbers and shred finely. Place strands in a colander and sprinkle with 1 tablespoon of vinegar. Let stand 40 minutes. Shake colander to remove excess liquid. Put into bowl and add chopped onions, clove of garlic, and chives. Combine remaining vinegar, stevia **or** xylitol, 2 tablespoons dill and water. Mix and pour over vegetables. Toss lightly with forks. Cover and refrigerate 15-30 minutes. Sprinkle with remaining dill.

Makes approximately 4-6 servings

Fresh Fruit Salad

Ingredients:
1 apple
1 banana
1 cup sweet cherries
1 peach
1 medium cantaloupe
1 medium honey dew melon
1 pint strawberries
1 quarter of a watermelon
2 tablespoons lemon juice
½ cup fresh orange juice

Directions:
Cut above fruits into a bowl. Mix lemon juice and orange juice. Pour over fruit and serve.

Makes approximately 8-10 servings

Green Pea Salad

Ingredients:

⅓ cup plain yogurt
1½ tablespoons Dijon mustard
⅛ teaspoon pepper
1 package (about 10 oz.) frozen tiny peas, thawed
1 hard-cooked large egg, chopped
½ cup red or green bell pepper, chopped
⅓ cup onion, thinly sliced
¼ cup celery, thinly sliced
6 lettuce leaves, rinsed and dried

Directions:

In a large bowl, stir together yogurt, mustard and pepper. Add peas, egg, bell pepper, onions and celery. Mix gently. Cover and refrigerate for at least 3 hours or up to 1 day.

To serve, line six individual plates with a lettuce leave. Spoon the salad mixture onto the lettuce.

Makes 6 servings

Pesto Pasta Salad

Ingredients:
1 cup dried tomatoes (not packed in oil)
2 tablespoons pine nuts
1 pound spelt medium size pasta shells **or** spelt elbow macaroni
1 cup firmly packed chopped fresh spinach
3 tablespoons dried basil
1 or 2 cloves garlic, peeled
⅓ cup grated Parmesan cheese
¼ cup olive oil
1 teaspoon sesame oil
Salt and pepper

Directions:
Place tomatoes in a small bowl and add boiling water to cover. Let stand until soft (about 10 minutes), stirring occasionally. Drain well; gently squeeze out excess liquid. Cut tomatoes into thin slivers and set aside.

While tomatoes are soaking, toast pine nuts in a small frying pan over medium heat until golden (about 3 minutes), stirring often. Pour out of pan and set aside.

In a 6-8 quart pan, bring 4 quarts of water to a boil over medium-high heat; stir in pasta and cook until just tender to bite, 8 to 10 minutes. (Or cook pasta according to package directions.) Drain, rinse with cold water until cool, and drain well again. Pour into a large serving bowl.

In a food processor or blender, whirl spinach, basil, garlic, cheese, olive oil, sesame oil, and 1 teaspoon water until smoothly puréed; scrape sides of container as needed and add a little more water if pesto is too thick.

Add tomatoes and spinach pesto to pasta; mix well. Sprinkle with pine nuts; season to taste with salt and pepper.

Makes 8 servings

Pineapple, Apple, & Strawberry Salad

Ingredients:
1 medium-size pineapple
1 small tart green-skinned apple
1 cup strawberries, coarsely chopped
⅓ cup plain yogurt
8 to 16 lettuce leaves, rinsed and dried
8 whole strawberries
1 cup small-curd cottage cheese

Directions:
Cut the peel and eyes from the pineapple. Slice off top third of pineapple; cut out and discard core, then chop fruit. Place chopped pineapple in a medium-size bowl and set aside. Cut remaining pineapple lengthwise into 8 wedges; cut off and discard core from each wedge. Core apple and cut into ½-inch chunks. Add apple, chopped strawberries, and yogurt to chopped pineapple; mix lightly.

On each of 8 individual plates, arrange 1 or 2 lettuce leaves, a pineapple wedge, a whole strawberry, eighth of the cottage cheese, and eighth of the fruit mixture.

Makes 8 servings

Spinach Salad with Garlic Croutons

Ingredients:

1½ pounds spinach stems removed, leaves rinsed and crisped
1 medium-size red onion, thinly sliced and separated into rings
8 ounces mushrooms, thinly sliced
1 large red bell pepper, seeded and thinly sliced
2 ounces feta cheese, crumbled
½ cup lemon juice
4 teaspoons olive oil
½ teaspoon dry oregano
2 cloves garlic, peeled
1 small loaf of spelt bread (see breads for recipe), cut into ½ inch thick slices

Directions:

Tear spinach leaves into bite-size pieces, if desired. Place spinach, onion, mushrooms, and bell pepper in a large bowl; set aside.

In a blender, whirl cheese, lemon juice, oil, oregano, and 1 clove of the garlic until smoothly blended, set aside.

Place spelt bread slices in a single layer on a baking sheet and broil about 5 inches below heat, turning once, until golden on both sides (about 4 minutes). Let toast slices cool briefly. Rub remaining garlic clove evenly over top of each toast slice; then discard garlic clove. (To save time, you can purchase croutons or a loaf of whole grain bread at your area health food store. Please make sure they have no bleached white or bleached wheat flour in them).

Pour dressing over salad and mix gently. Spoon salad onto individual plates. Arrange toasted croutons or bread slices atop salads (or arrange toast on a plate and serve on the side).

Makes 6 servings

Wilted Spinach Salad with Oranges

Ingredients:
2 medium-size oranges
2 quarts lightly packed spinach leaves, rinsed and crisped
1 large onion, thinly sliced and separated into rings
¼ cup balsamic or red wine vinegar
2 teaspoons peanut oil
1 teaspoon dried tarragon

Directions:
Grate 1 teaspoon peel (colored part only) from one of the oranges; set aside. With a sharp knife, cut remaining peel and all white membrane from both oranges. Holding fruit over a bowl to catch the juice, cut between membranes to free segments; place segments in bowl with juice and set aside. Place spinach in a large salad bowl.

In a wide frying pan, combine onion, vinegar, oil, tarragon and grated orange peel. Place over medium-low heat, cover, and cook until onions are tender-crisp when pierced (6 to 8 minutes). Gently stir in orange segments and juice. Pour orange mixture over spinach. Mix lightly, then serve at once.

Makes 4 servings

Warm Wild Rice & Asparagus Salad

Ingredients:
1 cup wild rice, rinsed and drained
1 cup lentils
1 pound mushrooms, thinly sliced
1 large onion, chopped
About 2½ cups vegetable stock (see recipe in soup section)
1 pound slender asparagus
3 tablespoons balsamic vinegar
1 tablespoon olive oil
½ cup grated Parmesan cheese

Directions:
In a 5 to 6 quart pan, combine rice and 8 cups of water. Bring to a boil over high heat; then reduce heat, cover, and simmer for 30 minutes. Meanwhile, sort through lentils, discarding any debris, rinse lentils, drain and set aside.

Add lentils to rice and continue to simmer until both rice and lentils are tender to bite (about 25 more minutes). Drain and let cool.

In a wide nonstick frying pan, combine mushrooms, onion, and ¼ cup of the broth. Cook over medium-high heat, stirring often, until liquid evaporates and browned bits stick to pan bottom (about 10 minutes). To deglaze pan, add ⅓ cup of the broth, stirring to loosen browned bits from pan; continue to cook until browned bits form again. Repeat deglazing step about 3 more times or until vegetables are browned, using ⅓ cup more broth each time.

Snap off and discard tough ends of asparagus; thinly slice stalks. Add asparagus and ⅓ cup more broth to mushroom mixture; cook, stirring often, until asparagus is tender-crisp to bite (about 2 minutes).

Spoon rice-lentil mixture into a large bowl. Add asparagus mixture, vinegar, and oil; mix gently but thoroughly. Sprinkle with cheese.

Makes 8 servings

Pasta

Fettuccine Alfredo

Ingredients:
2 cans (about 14 oz. each) artichoke hearts packed in water, drained and quartered
3 tablespoons parsley, chopped or dried
3 tablespoons green onions, thinly sliced
12 ounces dried spelt fettuccine
1 tablespoon butter or olive oil
3 cloves garlic, minced
1 tablespoon spelt flour (see glossary for definition)
1½ cups 2% milk
1 large package (about 8 oz.) nonfat cream cheese, cut into small chunks
1½ cups (about 4½ oz.) shredded Parmesan cheese
⅛ teaspoon ground nutmeg (optional)
Pepper

Directions:
In a medium-size bowl, combine artichokes, parsley, and onions. Set aside.

In a 5 to 6 quart pan, bring about 3 quarts of water to a boil over medium high heat; stir in spelt pasta and cook until just tender to bite, 8 to 10 minutes. (Or cook pasta according to package directions.) Drain well, return to pan, and keep hot.

Melt butter in a wide nonstick frying pan over medium heat. Add garlic and cook, stirring, until fragrant (about 30 seconds: do not scorch). Whisk in flour until well blended, then gradually whisk in milk. Cook, whisking, constantly, until mixture boils and thickens slightly (about 5 minutes). Whisk in cream cheese, 1 cup of Parmesan cheese, and nutmeg (if desired). Continue to cook, whisking constantly, until cheese is melted and evenly blended into sauce.

Working quickly, pour hot sauce over pasta and lift with 2 forks to mix. Spoon pasta into center of 4 shallow individual bowls. Then quickly arrange artichoke mixture around pasta. Sprinkle with remaining ½ cup Parmesan cheese, then with pepper. Serve immediately (sauce thickens rapidly and is absorbed quickly by pasta).

Makes 4 servings

Spelt Vegetable Lasagna

Ingredients:
1 teaspoon olive oil
1 zucchini, sliced
2 cups (16 oz.) reduced-fat ricotta cheese
1 egg
1 tablespoon dried basil
¼ teaspoon salt
⅛ teaspoon ground black pepper
2 cups tomato sauce (see recipe at end of this section)
9 spelt flour lasagna noodles, cooked
1 package (10 ounces) frozen chopped spinach, thawed and squeezed dry
¼ cup (1 ounce) grated Parmesan cheese
¼ cup (1 ounce) shredded mozzarella cheese

Directions:
Preheat the oven to 350°F. Coat a 13" x 9" baking dish with peanut oil cooking spray.

Heat the oil in a medium skillet over medium heat. Add zucchini and cook for 5 minutes, or until crisp-tender. Remove from the heat and set aside.

In a medium bowl, combine the ricotta cheese, egg, basil, salt and pepper. Set aside ½ cup of the spaghetti sauce.

Place 3 lasagna noodles in the prepared baking dish. Evenly spoon half of the spaghetti sauce over the noodles. Top with half of the ricotta mixture, half of the spinach, half of the zucchini, and half of the Parmesan. Repeat layering with 3 more noodles and the remaining ingredients. End with the remaining 3 noodles. Spoon the remaining sauce over top and sprinkle with the mozzarella.

Cover with foil and bake for 25 minutes. Uncover and bake for 20 minutes longer, or until hot and bubbly. Let stand for 10 minutes before serving.

Makes 12 servings

Pasta with Broccoli and Dried Tomatoes

Ingredients:
½ to ⅔ cup sliced sun-dried tomatoes (not oil-cured)
10 to 12 ounces of any spelt pasta, short chunky shape
2 to 3 good-size broccoli crowns cut into bite-size pieces
2½ tablespoons olive oil
½ cup grated fresh Parmesan cheese
Salt and pepper to taste

Directions:
Check the dried tomatoes when you remove them from the bag. If they are not moist, soak them in hot water for about 10 minutes and drain.

Cook the spelt pasta according to the package directions, drain.

Meanwhile, steam the broccoli in a covered saucepan on the stove top or in a covered microwave-safe container in the microwave, using a small quantity of water, until just a little beyond tender-crisp, drain.

Combine the cooked spelt pasta with the broccoli in a serving container. Add the oil, dried tomatoes, and Parmesan cheese and toss together. Season with salt and pepper and serve.

Makes 4 servings

Ricotta Spelt Pasta with Fresh Spinach

Ingredients:
12 ounces of spelt pasta (fettuccine, shells, etc.)
2 tablespoons butter
1 cup ricotta cheese
⅓ cup grated fresh Parmesan cheese
One 10 -12 ounce package fresh spinach, well washed and stemmed

Directions:
Cook the spelt pasta according to package directions, drain, reserving ½ cup of the hot pasta cooking water. Transfer the pasta to a serving container, toss with 1½ tablespoons of butter, and cover.

In a mixing bowl, combine the ricotta cheese with the reserved pasta cooking water and stir until well blended. Stir into the pasta along with the Parmesan cheese, and season with salt and pepper.

Cover and steam the spinach using just the water clinging to the leaves in the same pot used to cook the pasta. This should take only a minute or two. Drain the spinach well and chop coarsely. Transfer to a small serving bowl and toss with the remaining ½ tablespoon of butter. Serve at once, topping each serving with some of the steamed spinach.

Makes 4 servings

Marinated Spelt Pasta and Vegetables

Ingredients:
1 cup spelt elbow pasta
1 head broccoli, cut into small bite-sized pieces
1 small head of cauliflower, chop florets, discard stems and outside of head
¼ cup onion, chopped
2 tablespoons dry parsley
¼ cup pimiento, chopped
⅓ cup Parmesan cheese

SAUCE
½ cup canola oil
½ cup red wine vinegar
½ cup ketchup (See home-made ketchup recipe in condiment section)
½ teaspoon paprika
½ teaspoon dry mustard
½ teaspoon dried oregano

Directions:
Cook the spelt pasta according to the package directions. Drain well, rinse under cold running water, and drain again. Set aside.

To make the sauce, place all of the sauce ingredients in a 1 quart bowl, and blend well. Set aside.

Place the broccoli, cauliflower, onion, parsley, pimiento, and cheese in a 3 quart bowl, and toss to mix. Add the sauce, and toss well. Mix in the pasta gently, and toss well with two forks.

Cover the bowl and chill for at least 2-3 hours before serving.

Makes 4 servings

Summer Spelt Pasta Alfresco

Ingredients:

3 small tomatoes, peeled and chopped
1 cup thinly sliced onion
2 stalks celery, finely chopped
1 green bell pepper, finely chopped
1 zucchini, peeled and diced
2 cloves garlic, minced or pressed
3 tablespoons red wine vinegar
1 tablespoon xylitol (sugar) (see glossary for definition)
⅓ cup fresh basil leaves, chopped
1 teaspoon fresh rosemary, chopped
¾ teaspoon fresh oregano leaves, chopped
Coarsely ground pepper
8 ounces spelt rotelle (corkscrews), spelt ruote (wheels), or other spelt dry pasta shape
2 tablespoons grated Parmesan cheese

Directions:

Combine tomatoes, onion, celery, bell pepper, zucchini, garlic, vinegar, sugar, basil, rosemary, and oregano. Season to taste with pepper; mix well. Cover and refrigerate for at least 2 hours or up to 8 hours.

Shortly before serving, cook spelt pasta in 3 quarts boiling water in a 5 to 6 quart pan until done (7 to 9 minutes or according to package directions). Drain, rinse with cold water until cool, and drain again.

Transfer pasta to a serving bowl. Add tomato mixture and mix lightly. Sprinkle with Parmesan cheese and mix again.

Makes 4 servings

Pasta Pie

Ingredients:
½ cup low-fat milk
1 teaspoon cornstarch
2 large eggs
6 large egg whites
¾ cup shredded reduced-fat mozzarella cheese
¼ cup grated Parmesan cheese
2 tablespoons fresh oregano, chopped or 1½ tsp. dried oregano
2 cloves garlic, minced or pressed
¼ teaspoon salt
⅛ teaspoon crushed red pepper flakes
3 cups cold spelt spaghetti, cooked according to directions on box
1 teaspoon olive oil

TOMATO CREAM SAUCE
1 large can (about 28 oz.) dice tomatoes
½ cup reduced-fat sour cream
2 or 3 cloves garlic, peeled
2 teaspoons fresh thyme, chopped or ½ tsp. dried thyme
1 teaspoon xylitol (sugar) (see glossary for definition), or to taste
Salt and pepper to taste

Directions:
In a large bowl, combine milk and cornstarch; beat until smoothly blended. Add eggs and egg whites and beat well. Stir in mozzarella cheese, Parmesan cheese, chopped oregano, minced garlic, the ¼ teaspoon salt, and red pepper flakes. Add pasta to egg mixture; lift with 2 forks to mix well. Set aside.

Place a 9 inch round baking pan (do not use a nonstick pan) in oven while it heats to 500°F. When pan is hot (after about 5 minutes), carefully remove it from oven and pour in oil, tilting pan to coat. Mix pasta mixture again; then transfer to pan. Bake on lowest rack of oven until top of pie is golden and center is firm when lightly pressed (about 25 minutes).

To prepare tomato cream sauce, pour tomatoes and their liquid into a food processor or blender. Add sour cream, peeled garlic, thyme, and sugar; whirl until smoothly puréed. Season to taste with salt and pepper, set aside. Use at room temperature.

When pie is done, spread about ¾ cup of the sauce on each of the 4 individual plates. Cut pie into 4 wedges; place one wedge atop sauce on each plate. Offer remaining sauce to drizzle over pie.

Makes 4 servings

Spelt Penne Pasta with Turkey Sausage

Ingredients:
12 ounces spinach, stems removed, rinsed and drained
1 large red or yellow bell pepper, seeded
3 green onions
8 ounces spelt dried penne pasta
1 cup chicken stock (see recipe in soup section)
8 to 12 ounces mild or hot turkey Italian sausages, casings removed
½ cup balsamic vinegar
5 teaspoons xylitol (sugar), (see glossary for definition)
½ to ¾ teaspoon fennel seeds
Salt and pepper to taste

Directions:
Tear spinach into pieces. Cut bell pepper lengthwise into thin strips. Cut onions into 3 inch lengths and sliver lengthwise. Place vegetables in a large serving bowl and set aside.

Bring 8 cups water to a boil in a 4 to 5 quart pan over medium-high heat. Stir in spelt pasta and cook just until tender to bite (8 to 10 minutes); or cook according to package directions. Drain well and keep warm.

Chop or crumble sausages. Cook in a wide nonstick frying pan over medium-high heat, stirring often, until browned (about 10 minutes). Add vinegar and fennel seeds, stirring to loosen browned bits.

Add pasta to vegetables and immediately pour on sausage mixture; toss gently but well until spinach is slightly wilted. Serve immediately. Offer salt and pepper to taste.

Makes 6 servings

Spelt Rotini with Broccoli & Ricotta Cheese

Ingredients:
12 ounces dried spelt rotini or other spelt corkscrew-shaped pasta
2 tablespoons olive oil
5 green onions, thinly sliced
1 pound broccoli flowerets, cut into bite-size pieces
1½ cups ricotta cheese
Freshly grated Parmesan cheese
Coarsely ground pepper

Directions:
Bring 12 cups water to a boil in a 5 to 6 quart pan over medium-high heat. Stir in spelt pasta and cook until tender to bite (8 to 10 minutes); or cook according to package directions. Meanwhile, heat oil in a wide nonstick frying pan over medium-high heat. Add onions and cook, stirring, for 1 minute. Add broccoli and continue to cook, stirring, until bright green (about 3 minutes). Pour in ¼ cup of water and bring to a boil; reduce heat, cover, and simmer until broccoli is tender-crisp (about 5 minutes).

Drain pasta well, reserving ¼ cup of the water. Place in a serving bowl. Add vegetables and ricotta cheese. Mix thoroughly but gently; if too dry, stir in enough of the reserved water to moisten. Offer Parmesan cheese and pepper to taste.

Makes 4 servings

Spelt Ziti with Turkey, Feta Cheese and Sun-Dried Tomatoes

Ingredients
2 to 4 tablespoons sun-dried tomatoes in olive oil
½ cup chicken stock (see soup section for recipe)
2 tablespoons white vinegar
1 teaspoon cornstarch
1 small onion
8 ounces spelt ziti or penne pasta
2 turkey breast skinless tenderloins (about 1 lb. total), cut into ½ inch pieces
1½ teaspoons chopped fresh oregano or ½ tsp. dried oregano
1 large tomato, chopped and drained well
½ cup crumbled feta cheese

Drain sun-dried tomatoes well (reserve oil) and pat dry with paper towels. Then chop tomatoes and set aside.

To prepare sauce, in a small bowl, stir together soup stock, vinegar, and cornstarch until blended, set aside.

Chop onion and set aside

In a 4 to 5 quart pan, cook spelt pasta in about 8 cups of boiling water until just tender to bite (8 to 10 minutes). Drain pasta well and transfer to a warm large bowl, keep warm.

While pasta is cooking, measure 2 teaspoons of the oil from sun-dried tomatoes. Heat oil in a wide nonstick frying pan over medium-high heat. When oil is hot, add turkey and chopped oregano. Stir-fry just until meat is no longer pink in center , cut to test (2 to 3 minutes). Add water, 1 tablespoon at a time, if pan appears to be dry. Remove turkey with a slotted spoon, transfer to bowl with pasta and keep warm.

Add sun-dried tomatoes and onion to pan; stir-fry until onion is soft (about 4 minutes). Add water if pan is dry.

Stir reserved sauce well and pour into pan. Cook, stirring, until sauce boils and thickens slightly (1 to 2 minutes). Remove from heat and stir in fresh tomato. Spoon tomato mixture over pasta and turkey; mix gently but thoroughly.

Divide turkey mixture among 4 warm individual rimmed plates or shallow bowls. Sprinkle with feta cheese.

Makes 4 servings

Spelt Cheese Dumplings with Parsley

Ingredients:
1¼ cups white spelt flour (see glossary for definition)
¼ cup potato starch
½ teaspoon baking powder
¼ teaspoon salt
¼ cup softened butter
1 egg
⅓ cup low-fat milk
¾ tablespoon dried parsley
2 tablespoons grated parmesan or cheddar cheese

Directions:
Pour flour, potato starch, baking powder and salt in a 3 quart bowl. Mix well. Set aside.

In a 2 quart bowl, cream together the butter, egg, cheese (if desired) and milk. Slowly add the egg mixture to the flour mixture, beating the mixture with a fork until the batter begins to bubble. Stir in the parsley.

Place 2 quarts of water in a 3 quart pan and bring to a boil over high heat. Using a wet tablespoon, cut rounded spoonfuls of dough from the bowl, and drop the dough into the boiling water. After the dumplings have turned and risen to the top, reduce the heat to low, and simmer covered for 12 minutes. The dumplings are done when you test with a toothpick. Insert the toothpick into the center and pull it out. If it comes out clean, remove them from the water with a slotted spoon, and transfer to a serving bowl. Serve immediately.

Makes 12 dumplings

Spelt Drop Noodles

Ingredients:
2 eggs, beaten
½ cup vegetable stock (see soup section for recipe)
1½ cups spelt flour
Dash salt
Dash baking powder

Directions:
Place the eggs and vegetable stock in a 2 cup measuring cup and mix. Set aside.

Combine the flour, salt and baking powder in a 2 quart bowl. Slowly pour the egg mixture into the flour mixture, stirring continuously for about 2 minutes, or until the dough bubbles.

In a 3 quart saucepan, bring 2 quarts of water to a boil. Spoon enough of the dough onto a wet cutting board to make a circle about 6" in diameter. Tilt the board slightly over the pan of boiling water. As the dough runs towards the end of the board, use a sharp knife to quickly cut into the boiling water small (about 2½ x ¼") pieces of dough. Continue as quickly as possible until all the dough has been used. Reduce the heat to medium-low, and simmer for 10 minutes, or until noodles are no longer doughy inside when cut.

Drain the noodles well. If using the noodles immediately, toss with your favorite sauce and serve. If storing for later use, toss them with a small amount of vegetable stock or other liquid and refrigerate in an airtight container for up to 3 days.

Makes 4 servings

Basic Tomato Sauce

Ingredients:

¼ cup olive oil
1 large or 2 small onions, finely chopped
2 cloves garlic, minced
6 cans (16 ounce each) whole peeled tomatoes, diced
3 stalks celery, finely diced
1 green bell pepper, seeded, finely diced
1 carrot, finely grated
1 teaspoon dried thyme
2 tablespoon dried oregano
1 tablespoon dried basil
2 teaspoon zylitol (sugar) (see glossary for definition)
1 bay leaf
Dash black pepper
1 can tomato paste

Directions:

Place the olive oil in a 5-6 quart pan or dutch oven over medium heat. Add the onion and cook, stirring often, until the onion is soft. Add the garlic and continue to cook and stir for 1 minute.

Place the tomatoes, celery, green pepper, and carrot in a blender or food processor and purée for 1 minute, approximately or until the tomatoes are well blended.

Add the tomato mixture and all of the remaining ingredients to the onion mixture and stir well. Reduce the heat to low, and simmer the sauce for 2½ to 3 hours, stirring frequently.

Remove the bay leaf and discard. Add the tomato paste (This gives the sauce a thicker consistency). Use immediately or let the sauce cool and place in airtight containers. Refrigerate for up to 4-5 days or freeze for up to 3 months.

Makes 12 cups

Pizza

Basic Tomato Sauce

Ingredients:
¼ cup olive oil
1 large or 2 small onions, finely chopped
2 cloves garlic, minced
6 cans (16 ounce each) whole peeled tomatoes, diced
3 stalks celery, finely diced
1 green bell pepper, seeded, finely diced
1 carrot, finely grated
1 teaspoon dried thyme
2 tablespoon dried oregano
1 tablespoon dried basil
2 teaspoon zylitol (sugar) (see glossary for definition)
1 bay leaf
Dash black pepper
1 can tomato paste

Directions:
Place the olive oil in a 5-6 quart pan or dutch oven over medium heat. Add the onion and cook, stirring often, until the onion is soft. Add the garlic and continue to cook and stir for 1 minute.

Place the tomatoes, celery, green pepper, and carrot in a blender or food processor and purée for 1 minute, approximately or until the tomatoes are well blended.

Add the tomato mixture and all of the remaining ingredients to the onion mixture and stir well. Reduce the heat to low, and simmer the sauce for 2½ to 3 hours, stirring frequently.

Remove the bay leaf and discard. Add the tomato paste (This gives the sauce a thicker consistency). Use immediately or let the sauce cool and place in airtight containers. Refrigerate for up to 4-5 days or freeze for up to 3 months.

Makes 12 cups

Whole Wheat or White Spelt Pizza Dough

Ingredients:
1½ cups whole-wheat **or** white spelt flour
1 package dry yeast
¾ teaspoon salt
¼ teaspoon xylitol (sugar) (see glossary for definition)
½-⅔ cup hot water (120-130°F)
2 teaspoons olive oil

Directions:
Combine whole-wheat spelt flour **or** white spelt flour, yeast, salt and xylitol in a blender or food processor. Mix well. Combine hot water and oil in a measuring cup. With the motor running, gradually pour in enough of the hot liquid until the mixture forms a sticky ball. The dough should be quite soft. If it seems dry, add 1 to 2 tablespoons warm water; if too sticky, add 1 to 2 tablespoons spelt flour. Blend or process until the dough forms a ball. Blend or process for another 1 minute to knead.

Transfer the dough to a lightly spelt floured surface. Coat a sheet of plastic wrap with canola cooking spray and place it, sprayed side down, over the dough. Let the dough rest for 10 to 20 minutes before rolling.

Makes 1-12 ounce pizza crust

Broccoli & Black Olive Pizza

Ingredients:
Cornmeal for dusting
12 ounces Spelt Pizza Dough (See the beginning of this section for recipe)
2 cups broccoli florets, cut into ¾ inch pieces
½ cup red onion, diced
1 tablespoon plus 1 teaspoon olive oil
⅔ cup tomato sauce (see the beginning of this section for recipe)
¾ teaspoon dried oregano
⅛ teaspoon crushed red pepper
1 cup grated mozzarella cheese
¼ cup black olives, coarsely chopped

Directions:
Place a pizza stone or inverted baking sheet on the lowest oven rack; preheat oven to 500°F or highest setting. Coat a 12½ inch pizza pan with olive oil cooking spray and dust with cornmeal.

Prepare spelt pizza dough.

Place broccoli in a steamer basket over boiling water, cover and steam until just tender, 2 to 3 minutes. Rinse with cold water to stop cooking; drain well. Transfer to a medium bowl, add onion and 1 tablespoon olive oil; toss to coat.

Combine sauce, oregano and crushed red pepper.

On a lightly floured surface, roll the dough into a 13 inch circle. Transfer to the prepared pan. Turn edges under to make a slight rim. Brush the rim with the remaining 1 teaspoon olive oil.

Spread the sauce over the crust, leaving a ½ inch border. Sprinkle the mozzarella cheese. Scatter the broccoli mixture over the cheese. Sprinkle with olives.

Place the pizza pan on the heated pizza stone (or baking sheet) and bake the pizza until the bottom is crisp and golden, 10 to 14 minutes. Serve immediately.

Makes 4 slices

Broccoli and Sun-Dried Tomato Pizza (White or Red)

Ingredients:
¼ to ½ cup sliced sun-dried tomatoes (not oil-cured)
12 ounces Spelt Pizza Dough (see the beginning of this section for recipe)
1 cup tomato sauce (see the beginning of this section for recipe)
1 cup grated mozzarella cheese
1½ to 2 cups steamed bite-size broccoli florets

Directions:
If the dried tomatoes you are using are not moist, soak them in hot water for about 10 minutes, drain.

Preheat the oven to 425°F.

Place the crust on a pan, spread the sauce (red pizza) or ricotta cheese (white pizza) evenly over it, and sprinkle on the mozzarella cheese and broccoli florets.

Bake until the cheese is bubbly, 8 to 10 minutes. Remove from the oven, let stand 2 to 3 minutes, and cut into 4 to 6 wedges to serve.

Makes 4 to 6 servings

Vegetarian Pizza

Ingredients:
1 cup tomato sauce (see the beginning of this section for recipe)
12 ounces Spelt Pizza Dough (see the beginning of this section for recipe)
1 tablespoon olive oil
green pepper, chopped
onion, chopped
ripe tomato, diced
ripe olives, chopped
½ teaspoon thyme
2 basil leaves, chopped
1 package mozzarella cheese, grated

Directions:
Make spelt pizza dough and flatten out on pizza pan. Make a small rim all the way around the edge of the crust.

Brush 1 tablespoon olive oil over dough.

Pour on tomato sauce and spread on the crust.

Add green peppers, onion, tomato, olives, thyme, and basil.

Bake at 375°F for 15 minutes. Take out of oven and top with 1 package grated mozzarella cheese. Return to oven and bake another 15 minutes. Take out of oven and let cool for 2 minutes before serving.

Makes 4 to 6 servings

White Pizza Florentine

Ingredients:

10 to 12 ounces fresh spinach, well washed and stemmed
12 ounces Spelt Pizza Dough (see the beginning of this section for recipe)
1 cup ricotta cheese
1 cup part-skim mozzarella cheese
1 teaspoon dried oregano

Directions:

Preheat oven to 425°F.

Steam spinach in a large pot using only the water clinging to the leaves, until just wilted.

Make the Spelt Pizza Dough and place the crust on a pan, spreading it out over the pizza pan. Spread ricotta cheese evenly over it, followed by the spinach, mozzarella, and oregano.

Bake until the cheese is bubbly, 8 to 10 minutes. Remove from the oven, let stand for 2 to 3 minutes, and serve.

Makes 4 to 6 servings

Main Dishes & Sandwiches

Cheesy Brown Rice Pie

Ingredients:
¾ cup brown rice, cooked
8 ounces grated cheddar cheese
4 tablespoons grated parmesan cheese
2 spring onions, chopped
2 zucchini, grated
1 red pepper, grated
10 ounce can asparagus cuts, drained
10 ounces tomato sauce (see recipe in pasta section)
3 tablespoons pine nuts, toasted
3 eggs, lightly beaten
1 cup (6½ ounces) yogurt
Freshly ground black pepper

Directions:
Place cooked rice, cheddar cheese, parmesan cheese, spring onions, zucchini, red pepper, asparagus cuts, pine nuts, eggs, yogurt and black pepper to taste in a bowl and mix to combine.

Spoon rice mixture into a greased, deep sided 9 inch spring form tin and bake for 40 minutes or until firm. Allow to stand for 5 minutes in tin before turning out and serving. Cut into wedges and serve.

Makes 6 servings

Brown Rice, Vegetable & Herb Gratin

Ingredients:
3½ ounces brown rice
2 tablespoons butter
1 red onion, chopped
2 garlic cloves, crushed
1 carrot, cut into matchsticks
1 zucchini, sliced
2¾ ounces baby corn cobs, halved lengthwise
2 tablespoons sunflower seeds
3 tablespoons chopped mixed herbs
3½ ounces grated mozzarella cheese
2 tablespoons wholemeal breadcrumbs
salt and pepper

Directions:
Cook the rice in a saucepan of boiling salted water for 20 minutes or until cooked. Drain well.

Lightly grease a 1½ pint ovenproof dish.

Heat the butter in a frying pan. Add the onion and cook, stirring for 2 minutes or until softened.

Add the garlic, carrot, zucchini and corn cobs and cook for a further 5 minutes, stirring.

Mix the rice with the sunflower seeds and mixed herbs and stir into the pan.

Stir in half of the mozzarella cheese and season with salt and pepper to taste.

Spoon the mixture into the greased dish and top with the breadcrumbs and remaining cheese. Cook in a preheated oven at 350°F for 25-30 minutes or until the cheese begins to turn golden. Serve warm.

Makes 4 servings

Lemon-Basil Turkey with Roasted Vegetables

Ingredients:
Vegetable cooking spray
2 medium lemons
8 pounds turkey breast
1 tablespoon butter, melted
24 baby red or gold potatoes
1 pound butternut squash, peeled and cut into 1" cubes (about 3 cups)
12 small white boiling onions or 1 cup frozen whole onions
1 tablespoon dried basil leaves, crushed
1 cup chicken stock (see soup section for recipe)

Directions:
Spray 17" x 11" roasting pan with cooking spray.

Cut one lemon into thin slices. Juice remaining lemon and reserve 2 tablespoons juice. Loosen skin on turkey breast and place lemon slices under skin. Brush turkey with melted butter. Place turkey and vegetables in prepared pan. Sprinkle with basil. Mix broth and lemon juice. Pour half of broth mixture over turkey.

Roast at 375°F for one hour.

Stir vegetables. Add remaining broth mixture to pan. Roast 30 minutes or until turkey is no longer pink and vegetables are tender.

Makes 8 servings

Vegetable Curry Stir-Fry

Ingredients:

¾ pound red thin-skinned potatoes, cut into chunks
2 tablespoons olive oil
1 large onion, chopped
1 medium-size head cauliflower, cut into flowerets
½ pound green beans, cut into 2-inch pieces
2 medium-size carrots, sliced
2 tablespoons curry powder
½ cup water
8 ounces tomato sauce (see pasta section for recipe)
1 can (about 15½ ounces) garbanzo beans, drained and rinsed

Directions:

Place potatoes on a rack in a pan above 1 inch boiling water. Cover and steam over high heat until slightly tender when pierced (about 10 minutes). Lift out and set aside.

Heat olive oil in a wide frying pan over high heat. Add onion and cook, stirring, for 2 minutes. Add cauliflower, green beans, and carrots and cook, stirring, for 5 minutes. Add curry powder and water, stirring until vegetables are well coated. Stir in tomato sauce, garbanzo beans, and potatoes. Reduce heat, cover, and simmer until vegetables are tender (about 10 minutes).

Transfer to a serving dish.

Makes 4 to 6 servings

Vegetarian Chili

Ingredients:
1 cup dried red kidney beans (8 ounces), rinsed and picked over
1 tablespoon olive oil
1 medium red onion, chopped
2 cloves garlic, minced
1 green bell pepper, cut into ½-inch squares
1 pound sweet potatoes, peeled and cut into 1-inch chunks
1½ teaspoons chili powder
1 teaspoon salt
¾ teaspoon cinnamon
¾ teaspoon cumin
16 ounces tomato sauce (see pasta section for recipe)
1 package (10 ounces) frozen chopped spinach
1 package (10 ounces) frozen corn kernels (if tolerated)

Directions:
In medium saucepan, combine beans and cold water to cover by 2 inches. Bring to a boil and boil 2 minutes. Let stand for 1 hour; drain.

Return drained beans to saucepan. Add cold water to cover by 2 inches and bring to a boil. Reduce to a simmer, partially cover, and cook 1 hour or until beans are tender. Drain, reserving ½ cup bean cooking liquid.

Meanwhile, in Dutch oven or flameproof casserole, heat olive oil over medium-low heat. Add onion and garlic and cook, stirring frequently, for 7 minutes or until onion is tender. Add bell pepper and cook, stirring frequently, for 5 minutes or until tender.

Stir in sweet potatoes, chili powder, salt, cinnamon, and cumin until coated. Add tomato sauce and 1 cup of water and bring to a boil. Reduce to a simmer, cover and cook 20 minutes.

Stir in spinach, beans, and reserved bean cooking liquid. Return to a boil, reduce to a simmer, cover, and cook 20 minutes longer or until sweet potatoes are tender. Add corn (if tolerated) and cook for 5 minutes to heat through.

Makes 4 servings

Tailgate Chili

Ingredients:

2 cups small dried red beans (14 ounces)
2 tablespoons olive oil
2 medium onions, finely chopped
3 cloves garlic, finely chopped
1 red bell pepper, cut into ½-inch chunks
1 green bell pepper, cut into ½-inch chunks
1 tablespoon chili powder
2½ teaspoons ground cumin
1 can (28 ounces) tomatoes, chopped with their juice
¼ cup tomato paste
1½ teaspoons salt
1⅓ pounds ground turkey

Directions:

In large saucepan, combine beans and water to cover by 2 inches. Bring to a boil, reduce to a simmer, cover, and cook until beans are tender, about 1½ hours, adding more water if necessary to keep beans covered. When beans are tender, drain, reserving 1 cup of cooking liquid.

Meanwhile, in 4 quart Dutch oven, heat olive oil over medium heat. Add onion and garlic and cook, stirring frequently, 10 minutes or until onion is tender. Add bell peppers and cook 10 minutes or until bell peppers are tender.

Stir in chili powder, cumin, and cook 1 minute. Add tomatoes, tomato paste, salt, beans, and reserved bean cooking liquid and bring to a boil. Reduce to a simmer and cook uncovered 30 minutes or until chili is flavorful.

Crumble in turkey and cook, stirring frequently, 10 to 15 minutes or until turkey is cooked through and chili is lightly thickened.

Makes 8 servings

Mushroom, Spinach, and Cheddar Wraps

Ingredients:
8 to 10 ounces white, cremini, or baby bella mushrooms, cleaned and sliced
10 ounces fresh spinach, well washed, stemmed, and coarsely chopped.
Four 10-inch whole wheat wraps (non bleached flour)
1 cup grated sharp cheddar cheese

Directions:
Steam the mushrooms in a large skillet with enough water to keep the bottom moist. When they are tender, add the spinach, in batches if necessary, cover and cook, just until the spinach wilts down. Drain well.

Divide the mushroom-spinach mixture among the wraps, arranging it down the center of each. Sprinkle evenly with the cheese.

Briefly heat each wrap individually on a plate in the microwave or in a preheated 400° oven, just until heated through, and eat out of hand.

Makes 4 servings.

Tossed Salad Wraps

Ingredients:

3 cups thinly shredded lettuce
2 medium firm tomatoes, finely diced
½ medium green or red bell pepper, thinly sliced
¼ cup low-fat ranch, French or Thousand Island dressing
Four 10-inch whole wheat wraps (non bleached flour)

Directions:

Combine the first 4 ingredients in a mixing bowl and toss together.

Divide the salad among the 4 wraps, distributing it evenly over the entire surface, leaving approximately 2 inches empty at one side of each wrap. Roll up snugly. Cut each in half and eat out of hand.

Makes 4 servings

Brown Rice Turkey Burgers

Ingredients:
1 cup brown rice
1 pound ground turkey breast
2 tablespoons barbecue sauce (see recipe in condiment section)
1 egg beaten
4 cubes (1" each) cheddar cheese

Directions:
Preheat oven to 350°F.

Prepare brown rice according to package directions.

In a large bowl, combine the turkey, cooked brown rice, BBQ sauce, and egg. Divide the turkey mixture into 4 equal parts and shape into patties, placing a cube of cheese in the center of each patty.

Heat a large nonstick skillet over medium-high heat. Add the patties and sear on both sides. Place the patties in a nonstick baking pan and bake for 10 minutes, or until a thermometer inserted in the center of a pattie registers 165°F and the meat is no longer pink.

Serve alone or serve on spelt buns (see bread section for recipe).

Makes 4 servings

Poultry

Oven Fried Chicken with Almonds

Ingredients:

1 cup whole wheat bread crumbs
¼ cup grated parmesan cheese
¼ cup almonds, finely chopped
2 tablespoons parsley, chopped
1 clove garlic, crushed
1 teaspoon salt
¼ teaspoon dried thyme
Pinch of ground black pepper
¼ cup olive oil
2 pounds boneless, skinless chicken breasts, pounded to ½" thickness and cut into 12 pieces
Sprig parsley, for garnish

Directions:

Preheat oven to 400°F.

In a medium bowl, combine the bread crumbs, cheese, almonds, parsley, garlic, salt, thyme, and pepper. Mix thoroughly.

Place the oil in a shallow dish. Dip the chicken first in the oil, then roll in the crumb mixture. Place the chicken in a shallow baking pan.

Bake for 25 minutes, or until a thermometer inserted in the center of a piece of the chicken registers 170°F and the juices run clear. (Do not turn the chicken during cooking.) Garnish with the parsley.

Makes 6 servings

Garlic Chicken

Ingredients:
1 large clove garlic
½ teaspoon olive oil
4 boneless, skinless chicken breast halves (1½ pounds total)
1 teaspoon dried thyme
¼ teaspoon coarsely ground pepper
⅛ teaspoon salt
½ cup shredded mozzarella cheese

Directions:
Slice ½ inch off top of garlic. Then rub garlic with oil. Wrap garlic in foil and bake at 375°F until very soft when pressed (about 1¼ hours). Carefully remove garlic from foil; transfer to a rack and let stand until cool enough to touch (about 10 minutes).

Meanwhile, rinse chicken, pat dry, and sprinkle with chopped thyme and pepper. Place, skinned side up, in a lightly oiled 9 inch baking pan. Bake at 450°F until meat in thickest part is no longer pink; cut to test (12 to 15 minutes). Meanwhile, squeeze garlic clove from skins into a small bowl. Add salt; mash garlic thoroughly with a fork, incorporating salt.

Spread a fourth of the garlic mixture over each chicken piece; then sprinkle chicken with cheese. Return to oven; continue to bake just until cheese is melted and bubbly (about 3 more minutes).

Makes 4 servings

Honey Mustard Roast Chicken with Winter Vegetables

Ingredients:
6 small potatoes, cut into wedges
6 medium carrots, peeled, halved lengthwise and cut into 2-inch slices
3 medium parsnips, peeled, quartered lengthwise and cut into 2-inch slices
1 clove garlic, peeled
1 tablespoon olive oil
½ teaspoon salt
Fresh ground pepper to taste
2½-3 pounds boneless skinless chicken pieces
2 teaspoons rosemary, chopped
2 tablespoons Dijon mustard
1 tablespoon honey

Directions:
Preheat oven to 375°F. Coat a large roasting pan with peanut oil cooking spray.

Combine potatoes, carrots, parsnips, garlic, and oil in the roasting pan. Season with ¼ teaspoon salt and pepper and place in the center of the pan. Sprinkle with chopped rosemary.

Bake the chicken and vegetables for 20 minutes.

Meanwhile, in a small bowl, combine mustard and honey.

Turn chicken over and stir vegetables. Brush chicken with honey-mustard mixture. Continue roasting, stirring vegetables once or twice, until the chicken is cooked through and vegetables are tender, 25 to 35 minutes more. (If the chicken is done before the vegetables, remove and keep warm while vegetables finish cooking.) Serve immediately.

Makes 6 servings

Honeyed Chicken

Ingredients:
2 tablespoons sesame seeds
3 tablespoons honey
¼ cup dry sherry
¼ cup Dijon mustard
1 tablespoon lemon juice
3 whole chicken breasts (about 1 pound each), skinned, boned and split

Directions:
In a small frying pan, toast sesame seeds over medium heat, shaking pan often, until golden (about 3 minutes). Transfer to a small bowl and add honey, sherry, mustard, and lemon juice; stir until blended.

Arrange chicken breasts, slightly apart, in a 9 by 13 inch baking pan. Drizzle with honey mixture. Bake at 400°F, basting several times with sauce, until meat in thickest part is no longer pink; cut to test (15 to 20 minutes). Transfer chicken to individual plates. Offer with any remaining sauce.

Makes 6 servings

Lemon Chicken

Ingredients:

5 or 6 large lemons
¾ cup plus 1 tablespoon cornstarch
⅓ cup chicken stock (see soup section for recipe)
¼ cup xylitol (sugar) (see glossary for definition)
2 tablespoons light corn syrup
2 tablespoons white vinegar
1 tablespoon plus 1 teaspoon olive oil
½ teaspoon salt
2 cloves garlic, minced or pressed
2 large egg whites
¼ cup white spelt flour
1 teaspoon baking powder
1 teaspoon finely minced fresh ginger
⅛ teaspoon ground pepper
1 pound skinless, boneless chicken breast, cut into ½ by 3 inch strips
Finely shredded lemon peel

Directions:

To prepare sauce, finely shred enough peel (colored part only) from 1 or 2 of the lemons to make ½ teaspoon; set aside. Squeeze enough juice to measure 3 tablespoons. In a small bowl, stir together lemon juice and 1 tablespoon of the cornstarch until blended. Stir in lemon peel, chicken stock, xylitol, corn syrup, vinegar, 1 tablespoon water, 1 teaspoon of the oil, ¼ teaspoon of the salt, and garlic. Set sauce aside.

Thinly slice the remaining lemons and place slices on a rimmed platter, overlapping them, if necessary; cover and set aside.

In a large bowl, beat egg whites and ½ cup water to blend. Add remaining ¾ cup cornstarch, flour, baking powder, ginger, remaining ¼ teaspoon salt, and pepper; stir until smoothly blended.

Heat remaining 1 tablespoon oil in a wide nonstick frying pan over medium-high heat. Meanwhile, dip chicken pieces in egg-white batter. Lift out and drain briefly to let excess batter drip off; discard remaining batter.

When oil is hot, add chicken and stir-fry gently, separating pieces, until meat is lightly browned on outside and no longer pink in center; cut to test (5 to 7 minutes; if any pieces brown too much, remove them from pan and keep warm). Arrange chicken over lemon slices on platter; keep warm.

Wipe pan clean (be careful; pan is hot). Stir reserved lemon sauce well; pour into pan. Stir over medium-high heat until sauce boils and thickens slightly (1 to 2 minutes). Pour sauce over chicken and sprinkle with additional shredded lemon peel.

Makes 4 servings

Peanut Chicken with Rice

Ingredients:
1 cup brown rice
1 package (about 10 ounces) frozen tiny peas, thawed and drained
3 tablespoons crunchy or smooth peanut butter
3 tablespoons no sugar plum or grape jelly
1 tablespoon xylitol (sugar) (see glossary for definition)
1½ teaspoons lemon juice
1½ teaspoons soy sauce
1 teaspoon sesame oil
2 teaspoons olive oil mixed with teaspoon ground ginger
1 pound skinless, boneless chicken breast, cut into 54-inch pieces
2 tablespoons sliced onion
lemon wedges

Directions:
In a 3 to 4 quart pan, bring 2 cups water to a boil over high heat; stir in rice. Reduce heat, cover and simmer until liquid has been absorbed and rice is tender to bite (about 20 minutes). Stir peas into rice; remove from heat and keep warm. Fluff occasionally with a fork.

While rice is cooking, prepare sauce. In a small bowl, stir together peanut butter, jam, 2 tablespoons water, lemon juice, soy sauce, and sesame oil. Set aside.

Heat ginger oil in a wide nonstick frying pan over medium-high heat. When oil is hot, add chicken and stir-fry until no longer pink in center; cut to test (4 to 6 minutes). Remove chicken from pan with a slotted spoon and keep warm. Discard drippings from pan and wipe pan clean (be careful; pan is hot).

Stir sauce well and pour into pan. Stir over medium heat just until smoothly blended and heated through. Add chicken and onion; remove pan from heat and stir to coat chicken and onion with sauce.

Spoon rice mixture onto a rimmed platter and top with chicken mixture. Offer lemon wedges to squeeze over stir-fry to taste.

Makes 4 servings

Sautéed Turkey with Provolone and Sage

Ingredients:
1 pound thinly sliced turkey breast
2 teaspoons dried sage
2 teaspoons olive oil
½ cup finely shredded provolone or mozzarella cheese
pepper to taste
lemon wedges
salt to taste

Directions:
Rinse turkey and pat dry. Sprinkle one side of each slice with dried sage; set aside.

Heat 1 teaspoon of the oil in a wide nonstick frying pan over medium-high heat. Add half the turkey, sage-coated side down, and cook until golden on bottom (about 1½ minutes). Then turn pieces over and continue to cook until no longer pink in center; cut to test (30 to 60 more seconds). Transfer cooked turkey to a platter and sprinkle with half the cheese. Cover loosely with foil and keep warm.

Repeat to cook remaining turkey; using remaining 1 teaspoon oil, add water, 1 tablespoon at a time, if pan appears dry. Transfer turkey to platter; sprinkle with remaining cheese.

Sprinkle turkey with pepper, salt, and lemon to taste.

Makes 4 servings

Sesame Chicken with Stir-Fry Vegetables

Ingredients:

4 chicken breast halves (about 2 pounds total) skinned and boned
1 teaspoon sesame seeds
Canola oil cooking spray
4 teaspoons vinegar
4 teaspoons soy sauce
1½ teaspoons sesame oil
1 tablespoon grated fresh ginger
2 cloves garlic, minced or pressed
½ teaspoon xylitol (sugar) (see glossary for definition)
1 tablespoon canola oil
9 ounces mushrooms, sliced
4 cups thinly sliced red cabbage
4 ounces snow peas, ends and strings removed
2 cups hot cooked brown rice

Directions:

Rinse chicken, pat dry, and sprinkle with sesame seeds. Spray a ridge cook top grill pan with cooking spray. Place over medium heat and preheat until a drop of water dances on the surface. Then place chicken on grill and cook, turning once, until well browned on outside and no longer pink in thickest part; cut to test (12 to 15 minutes).

Meanwhile, in a small bowl, stir together vinegar, soy sauce, sesame oil, ginger, garlic, and xylitol; set aside. Then heat canola oil in a wide nonstick frying pan over medium-high heat.

Add mushrooms and cook, stirring often, for about 3 minutes. Add cabbage and cook, stirring often, until it begins to soften (about 2 minutes). Add pea pods and cook, stirring, just until they turn bright green (1 to 2 minutes). Add vinegar mixture and stir for 1 more minute.

Divide vegetables among 4 warm dinner plates. Cut each chicken piece diagonally across the grain into ½ inch-wide strips. Arrange chicken over vegetables; serve with rice.

Makes 4 servings

Seafood

Sautéed Flounder with Orange-Shallot Sauce

Ingredients:

⅓ cup spelt flour
½ teaspoon salt, or to taste
pepper to taste
1 pound flounder, sole **or** haddock fillets
1 tablespoon olive oil
1 large shallot, finely chopped (about ⅓ cup)
½ cup dry white wine
1 cup freshly squeezed orange juice
2 heaping teaspoons Dijon mustard
2 teaspoons butter
2 tablespoons fresh parsley, chopped

Directions:

Mix flour, salt and pepper in a shallow bowl. Thoroughly dredge fish fillets in the mixture.

Heat oil in a large nonstick skillet over medium-high heat until hot but not smoking. Add the fish and cook until lightly browned or just opaque in the center, 3 to 4 minutes per side. Transfer to a plate and cover loosely with foil.

Add shallot to the pan and cook over medium-high heat, stirring often, until softened and beginning to brow, about 3 minutes. Add wine and bring to a simmer, scraping up any browned bits. Cook until most of the liquid has evaporated, 1 to 2 minutes. Add orange juice and mustard; bring to a boil. Reduce heat to low and simmer until the sauce thickens a bit, about 5 minutes. Add butter and parsley; stir until the butter is melted. Transfer fish to individual plates, top with sauce and serve.

Makes 4 servings

Halibut with Tomatoes & Dill

Ingredients:

1 pound cherry tomatoes cut into halves
½ cup green onion, thinly sliced
2 cloves garlic, minced or pressed
½ teaspoon dry dill weed
2 teaspoons olive oil
2 tablespoons water
1½ pounds halibut or cod fillets
2 tablespoons lemon juice

Directions:

Arrange tomatoes, cut side up, in a 9" x 13" baking pan. In a small bowl, mix onions, garlic, dill weed, oil and water. Distribute onion mixture over tomatoes. Bake on top rack of oven at 425°F for 25 minutes.

Rinse fish and pat dry; then cut into 4 equal pieces, if necessary. Place fish in a baking pan large enough to hold pieces in a single layer. Drizzle the lemon juice, cover, and place in oven, setting pan on bottom of oven rack.

Continue to bake fish and tomatoes until tomatoes are lightly browned on top and fish is just opaque but still moist in thickest part; cut to test (8 to 10 minutes).

Transfer fish to a platter. Add fish cooking juices to tomato mixture and stir well; spoon over fish.

Makes 4 servings

Easy Salmon Cakes

Ingredients for Salmon Cakes:

3 teaspoons olive oil, divided
1 small onion, finely chopped
1 stalk celery, finely diced
2 tablespoons fresh parsley, chopped
15 ounces canned salmon, drained, or 1½ cups cooked salmon
1 large egg, lightly beaten
1½ teaspoons Dijon mustard
1¾ cups fresh whole-wheat breadcrumbs
½ teaspoon pepper
Creamy Dill Sauce (recipe follows)
1 lemon, cut into wedges

Directions for Salmon Cakes:

Preheat oven to 450°F. Coat a baking sheet with canola oil cooking spray.

Heat 1½ teaspoons olive oil in a large nonstick skillet over medium-high heat. Add onion and celery; cook, stirring, until softened, about 3 minutes. Stir in parsley; remove from the heat.

Place salmon in a medium bowl. Flake apart with a fork; remove any bones and skin. Add egg, breadcrumbs and mustard; mix well. Shape the mixture in 8 patties, about 2½ inches wide.

Heat remaining 1½ teaspoons oil in the skillet over medium heat. Add 4 patties and cook until the undersides are golden, 2 to 3 minutes. Using a wide spatula, turn them over onto the prepared baking sheet. Repeat with the remaining patties.

Bake the salmon cakes until golden on top and heated through, 15 to 20 minutes. Meanwhile, prepare Creamy Dill Sauce. Serve with sauce and lemon wedges.

Ingredients for Dill Sauce:

¼ cup mayonnaise (see recipe in condiment section)
¼ cup plain yogurt
2 scallions, thinly sliced
1 tablespoon lemon juice
1 tablespoon fresh dill, finely chopped
freshly ground pepper to taste

Directions for Dill Sauce:

Combine ingredients in a small bowl and mix well. Serve salmon cakes with sauce.

Makes about ½ cup

Mustard Crusted Salmon

Ingredients:
1¼ pounds center-cut salmon fillets cut into 4 portions
¼ teaspoon salt, or to taste
freshly ground pepper to taste
¼ cup sour cream
2 tablespoons mustard
2 teaspoons lemon juice
Lemon wedges to garnish

Directions:
Preheat broiler. Line a broiler pan or baking sheet with foil, then coat it with canola oil cooking spray.

Place salmon pieces, skin-side down, on the prepared pan. Season with salt and pepper. Combine sour cream, mustard and lemon juice in a small bowl and spread evenly over the salmon.

Broil the salmon 5 inches from the heat source until it is opaque in the center, 10 to 12 minutes. Serve with lemon wedges.

Makes 4 servings

Garlic Shrimp with Rice

Ingredients:
2 teaspoons butter
2 teaspoons olive oil
3 tablespoons water
3 cloves garlic, minced or pressed
1 pound large shrimp, shelled and deveined (about 25 per pound)
About 4 cups brown rice, cooked and hot
Lemon wedges
Salt and pepper to taste
Dry parsley for garnish

Directions:
Melt butter in a wide nonstick frying pan over medium-high heat.

Add oil, garlic, 3 tablespoons water and shrimp. Cook, stirring, until shrimp are just opaque but still moist in the center; cut to test (3 to 4 minutes).

To serve, spoon cooked, hot brown rice onto a platter or 4 dinner plates; Spoon shrimp and pan juices over rice. Sprinkle with dry parsley for garnish. Salt and pepper to taste. Serve with lemon wedges.

Makes 4 servings

Sole Florentine

Ingredients:

6 thin sole fillets (about 3 ounces each)
2 pounds spinach, stems removed, leaves rinsed and coarsely chopped
¼ teaspoon ground nutmeg
2 tablespoons lemon peel, grated
2 tablespoons fresh parsley, chopped
½ cup chicken stock (see soup section for recipe)
1 small dry bay leaf
4 whole black peppercorns

Directions:

Rinse fish and pat dry. Trim each fillet to make a 3" by 8" rectangle (reserve trimmings); set aside. Finely chop trimmings; place in a bowl and add 1½ cups of the spinach, nutmeg, lemon peel, and parsley. Mix well.

Spread spinach mixture evenly over fillets. Gently roll up fillets and secure with toothpicks.

Place fish rolls, seam side down, in a 9-inch baking dish. Pour broth around fish; add bay leaf and peppercorns. Cover and bake in a 400°F oven for 10 minutes.

Place remaining spinach in another 9-inch baking dish. With a slotted spoon, lift fish rolls from the first baking dish; arrange atop spinach (discard poaching liquid). Cover and bake until fish is just opaque but still moist in thickest part; cut to test (about 7 minutes). Remove and discard toothpicks from fish.

Makes 6 servings

Sole with Herbs

Ingredients:
2 pounds boneless, skinless sole fillets
½ cup chicken stock (see soup section for recipe)
¼ cup shallots, minced
1 tablespoon fresh tarragon, thyme **or** sage, chopped
6 to 8 thin lemon slices
6 to 8 tarragon, thyme, or sage sprigs
2 teaspoons cornstarch blended with 1 tablespoon cold water
salt and pepper

Directions:
Rinse fish and pat dry. Then arrange fillets, overlapping slightly, in a 9" by 13" baking dish. Pour chicken stock over fish; sprinkle with shallots and chopped tarragon, thyme **or** sage. Lay lemon slices and tarragon, thyme **or** sage sprigs on fish. Bake in a 375°F oven until fish is just opaque but still moist in thickest part; cut to test (about 15 minutes).

Keeping fish in dish, carefully spoon off pan juices into a small pan. Cover fish and keep warm. Bring pan juices to a boil over high heat; then boil, uncovered, until reduced to ¾ cup (about 5 minutes). Stir in cornstarch mixture; bring to a boil, stirring. Season sauce to taste with salt and pepper, then pour over fish.

Makes 6 servings

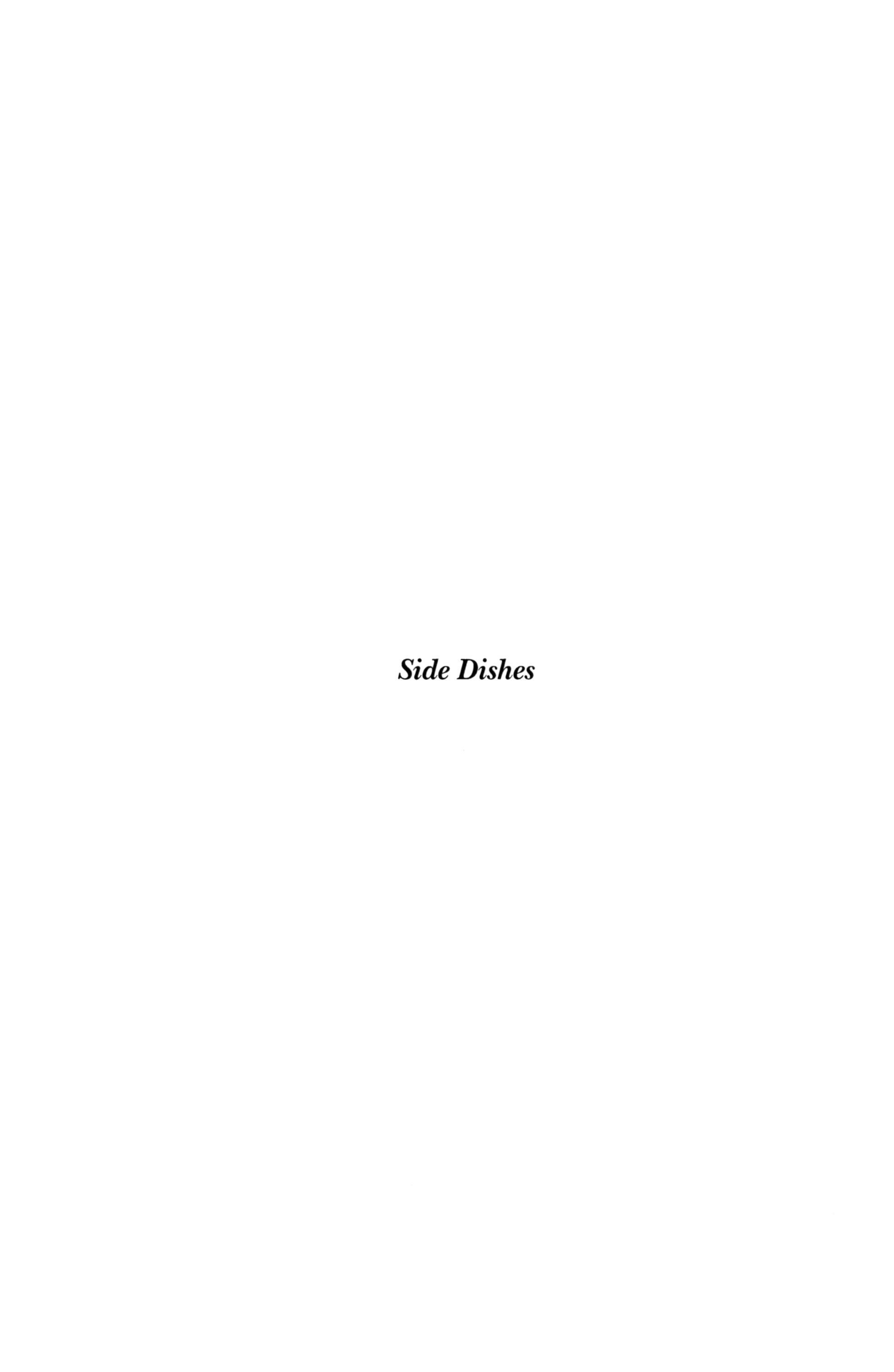

Side Dishes

Gingered Asparagus

Ingredients:
1 pound asparagus, tough ends snapped off, cut diagonally into 2 inch pieces
1 tablespoon fresh ginger, minced
3 tablespoons lemon juice
2 teaspoons sesame oil

Directions:
Place asparagus on a rack in a pan above 1 inch boiling water. Cover and steam over high heat until tender-crisp (5-7 minutes).

Transfer to a bowl and add ginger, lemon juice, and oil. Stir well. Serve warm or at room temperature.

Makes 4 servings

Curry-Glazed Carrots

Ingredients:
1 tablespoon orange peel, grated
¾ cup orange juice
2 tablespoons maple syrup
2 teaspoons cornstarch blended with 2 tablespoons cold water
1 teaspoon curry powder
1¼ pounds carrots, cut diagonally into ¼-inch slices
2 tablespoons parsley, minced
salt and pepper

Directions:
In a bowl, stir together orange peel, orange juice, syrup, and cornstarch mixture; set aside.

In a wide nonstick frying pan, stir curry powder over medium-high heat just until fragrant (about 30 seconds; do no scorch). Add carrots and ⅓ cup water. Cover and cook just until carrots are tender when pierced (about 4 minutes). Uncover and stir-fry until liquid has evaporated.

Stir orange juice mixture well; then pour into pan and cook, stirring, until sauce boils and thickens slightly. Pour carrots and sauce into a serving bowl and sprinkle with parsley. Season to taste with salt and pepper.

Makes 4 servings

Broccoli & Cheddar-Stuffed Potatoes

Ingredients:
4 large baking potatoes
¼ cup 2% milk
2 cups broccoli florets, finely chopped, steamed
1 cup grated cheddar cheese

Directions:
Bake or microwave the potatoes until done but still firm. When cool enough to handle, cut each in half lengthwise. Scoop out the inside of each potato half, leaving a sturdy shell, about ¼ inch thick all around.

Transfer the scooped-out potato to a mixing bowl and mash it coarsely. Add the remaining ingredients and stir well to combine.

Stuff the mixture back into the potato shells. Heat as needed in the microwave or in a preheated 400°F oven, and serve.

Makes 4 servings

Cauliflower & Broccoli with Herb Sauce

Ingredients:
2 small cauliflowers
8 ounces broccoli
salt and pepper to taste

Directions:
Cut the cauliflowers in half and the broccoli into very large florets. Cook the cauliflower and broccoli in a saucepan of boiling salted water for 10 minutes. Drain well and transfer to a shallow ovenproof dish.

Sauce Ingredients:
8 tablespoons olive oil
4 tablespoons butter
2 teaspoons grated ginger
2 lemons, rind and juice
5 tablespoons chopped coriander
5 tablespoons grated cheddar cheese

Sauce Directions:
To make the sauce, put the oil and butter in a pan and heat gently until the butter melts. Add the ginger, lemon juice and rind and coriander and simmer for 2 to 3 minutes.

Pour the sauce over the vegetables in the dish and sprinkle the cheese on top. Cook under a hot grill for 2-3 minutes or until the cheese is bubbling and serve immediately.

Makes 4 servings

Orange-Ginger Green Beans

Ingredients:
1 pound green beans
1 tablespoon butter
½ cup chopped shallots
1 tablespoon fresh ginger, finely chopped
½ teaspoon orange peel, grated

Directions:
Bring a medium saucepan of water to a boil over medium-high heat. Add the beans, cover, and simmer for 5 minutes, or until tender. Drain and remove to a bowl.

Melt the butter in the same pan over low heat. Add the shallots and ginger and sauté for 5 minutes, or until the shallots are tender. Add the beans and orange peel and toss to combine.

Makes 8 servings

Cheese & Potato Layer Bake

Ingredients:
1 pound potatoes
1 leek, sliced
3 garlic cloves, crushed
1¾ ounces cheddar cheese, grated
1¾ ounces mozzarella, grated
1 ounce parmesan cheese, grated
2 tablespoons parsley, chopped
¼ pint single cream
¼ pint milk
salt and pepper to taste
fresh parsley, chopped to garnish (leaves only)

Directions:
Cook the potatoes in a saucepan of boiling salted water for 10 minutes. Drain well. Cut the potatoes into thin slices. Arrange a layer of potatoes in the base of an ovenproof dish. Layer with a little of the leek, garlic, cheese and parsley. Season well.

Repeat the layers until all of the ingredients have been used, finishing with a layer of cheese on top.

Mix the cream and milk together, season and pour over the potato layers. Cook in a preheated oven at 325°F, for 1-1¼ hours or until golden brown and bubbling and the potatoes are cooked through. Garnish and serve.

Makes 4 servings

Mashed Garlicky Potatoes

Ingredients:
3¼ pounds russet potatoes (4-5 large potatoes), peeled and cut into 2-inch pieces
4 large cloves garlic, peeled
2 tablespoons butter
½ teaspoon salt, or to taste
pepper to taste

Directions:
Place potatoes and garlic in a large pot, cover with lightly salted water and bring to a boil. Cover and cook over medium heat until the potatoes are tender, about 20 minutes. Drain, reserving cooking liquid.

Return the potatoes and garlic to the pot. Add butter. Mash potatoes with a potato masher, adding ½ to 1 cup of the reserved liquid to make a creamy consistency. Season with salt and pepper. Transfer the mashed potatoes to a warmed serving bowl.

Makes 8 servings

Herbed Packet Potatoes

Ingredients:
2 tablespoons butter
1 tablespoon fresh parsley, chopped
½ teaspoon fresh lemon peel, grated
½ teaspoon salt
⅛ teaspoon pepper
1½ pounds small red potatoes, cut in half

Directions:
Preheat oven to 450°F. In a 3 quart saucepan, melt butter with parsley, lemon peel, salt and pepper over medium-low heat. Remove saucepan from heat; add potatoes and toss well to coat.

Place potato mixture in center of 24" by 18" sheet of heavy-duty foil. Fold edges over and pinch to seal tightly.

Place package on a rimmed cookie sheet or baking dish and bake until potatoes are tender when potatoes are pierced (through foil) with knife, about 30 minutes.

Makes 6 servings

Italian Oven Fried Potatoes

Ingredients:
2 pounds red thin-skinned potatoes, scrubbed and cut into 1-inch chunks
1 to 2 tablespoons olive oil
2 teaspoons dry oregano
2 teaspoons dry basil
1 clove garlic, minced or pressed
⅓ cup grated parmesan cheese
salt to season

Directions:
In a 10-inch by 15-inch rimmed baking pan, mix potatoes and oil. Bake at 475°F oven until potatoes are, richly browned (35 to 45 minutes). After potatoes have begun to brown (but not before then), turn them over several times with a wide spatula.

Transfer potatoes to a serving bowl and sprinkle with dry oregano and basil, garlic, and 3 tablespoons of the cheese. Stir to mix; season to taste with salt. Top with remaining cheese.

Makes 4 servings

Scalloped Potatoes

Ingredients:
6 medium potatoes
3 tablespoons butter
2 tablespoons cornstarch
2½ cups 2% milk
¼ cup onion, chopped
¼ cup green pepper, chopped
1 pound turkey bacon, cooked until crisp, broken into small pieces
1 tablespoon butter

Directions:
Peel and slice potatoes.

Melt 3 tablespoons butter in a saucepan, adding the corn starch, salt and pepper.

Cook until bubbly. Slowly add the milk, heating until thickened, stirring constantly.

Cook 1 pound of turkey bacon until crisp and break into small pieces.

Layer vegetables, bacon and sauce into casserole dish. Dot 1 tablespoon butter over top of vegetables.

Cover and bake at 350°F, approximately 40 minutes.

Makes 6 servings

Spinach Casserole

Ingredients:
2 packages frozen chopped spinach
2½ tablespoons chopped onion
2 eggs, beaten
1 cup parmesan cheese
8 ounces sour cream
1½ cups spelt spaghetti, cooked

Directions:
Combine all of the above ingredients in a casserole dish. Mix well. Bake at 350°F until bubbly.

Makes 4 servings

Candied Sweet Potatoes

Ingredients:
2 tablespoons butter, melted
Juice of 2 oranges (½ to ¾ cup)
⅓ cup maple syrup
1 teaspoon pumpkin pie spice **or** 1 teaspoon cinnamon
5 large sweet potatoes, peeled and sliced ¼ inch thick

Directions:
Preheat oven to 375°F.

Combine the first four (4) ingredients in a large mixing bowl. Stir until well combined. Add the sliced potatoes, stir well, and transfer to a shallow 1½ quart round or 9" by 13" oblong baking dish.

Cover and bake until the sweet potatoes are just tender, about 40 minutes. Stir once or twice during the time to distribute the liquid over the potatoes. Bake, uncovered, until the glaze thickens, an additional 10 to 15 minutes. Cover and keep warm until ready to serve.

Makes 6 servings

Desserts

Jam Filled Almond Cookies

Ingredients:

1½ cups sliced almonds
1 cup xylitol (sugar) (see glossary for definition)
1⅔ cup spelt flour (see glossary for definition)
1 teaspoon ground cinnamon
2 tablespoons butter, cut into small pieces
4 ounces cream cheese, cut into small pieces
¼ cup unsweetened applesauce
⅔ cup no sugar apricot **or** raspberry jam

Directions:

Pulse almonds, sugar, spelt flours and cinnamon in a food processor or blender until finely ground. Add butter and cream cheese; pulse until the mixture resembles coarse meal. Add applesauce and pulse until the mixture begins to form a ball, about 45 seconds.

Lightly sprinkle a work surface with spelt flour; remove the dough from the processor or blender and knead briefly. Divide the dough in half and shape each piece into a disk. Wrap in plastic and refrigerate until firm, at least 1 hour.

Position rack in center of oven; preheat to 350°F. Coat 3 baking sheets with canola cooking spray.

Lightly dust the dough with spelt flour. Roll out each piece between sheets of lightly spelt floured wax paper to an even ⅛-inch thickness. Transfer the dough, still in wax paper, to a baking sheet. Chill in the freezer until firm, about 20 minutes.

Working with one piece of dough at a time, use a 2½-inch fluted round cutter to cut out cookies. For half of the cookies, use a 1-inch round or star cutter to cut out a hole in the center. Reroll and cut scraps. Place cookies 1 inch apart on prepared baking sheets.

Bake the cookies one sheet at a time until set and very lightly browned, 10 to 20 minutes. Set baking sheets on wire racks and cool completely.

To assemble cookies, spread a rounded teaspoon of jam in the center of each solid cookie. Place the smaller cookies with the holes on top of the cookies with jam.

Makes about 2½ dozen cookies

Baked Apples with Yogurt

Ingredients:
6 medium sweet cooking apples, such as Cortland
⅓ cup xylitol (sugar) (see glossary for definition)
1 teaspoon cinnamon
¼ cup walnuts, finely chopped (optional)
1 cup vanilla yogurt

Directions:
Preheat the oven to 350°F

Core the apples carefully with a small sharp knife or apple corer, and place them in a baking pan.

Combine the xylitol and cinnamon and optional walnuts in a small bowl and stir together. Divide the mixture among the hollows of each apple.

Fill the baking pan with about ½ inch of water. Cover with foil and bake until the apples are tender, about 45 minutes.

Allow the apples to cool until just warm, fill the hollows with a little yogurt, and serve.

Makes 6 servings

Apple & Almond Soufflé

Ingredients:

3 medium baking apples, peeled, cored, and cut into bite-size pieces
¼ cup water
3 tablespoons xylitol (sugar) (see glossary for definition)
½ teaspoon almond extract
5 egg whites
¼ cup almonds, sliced and toasted (optional)

Directions:

In a 2-quart saucepan, combine the apples and water. Bring to a boil over high heat. Reduce the heat to low, cover, and simmer, stirring occasionally, for 10 minutes, or until the apples are tender. Stir in the sugar substitute and almond extract. Remove from the heat and place in the refrigerator for 10 minutes. (Place a hot pad underneath the pot in the refrigerator).

Preheat the oven to 425°F.

In a large bowl, with an electric mixer on high speed, beat the egg whites until stiff peaks form. With a rubber spatula, gently fold into the cooled apple mixture. Spoon the mixture into a 1½-quart soufflé dish.

Bake for 15 minutes, or until the soufflé is puffed and browned.

Sprinkle with almonds before serving, if using. Serve warm.

Makes 4 servings

Baked Apples with Oatmeal Streusel

Ingredients:
4 large Rome **or** Cortland apples (10 ounces each)
¼ cup brown sugar, packed
¼ cup quick-cooking oats, uncooked
2 tablespoons chopped dates
½ teaspoon ground cinnamon
2 teaspoons butter

Directions:
Core apples, cutting out a 1¼-inch diameter cylinder from center of each, almost but not all the way through to bottom. Remove peel about one-third of the way down from the top. Place apples in shallow 1½-quart ceramic casserole or 8" by 8" glass baking dish.

In a small bowl, combine brown sugar, oats, dates, and cinnamon. Fill each cored apple with equal amounts of oat mixture. (Mixture will spill over top of apples.) Place ½ teaspoon of butter on top of the filling in each apple.

Microwave apples, covered, on medium-high until tender, 12-14 minutes, turning each apple halfway through cooking time. Spoon cooking liquid from baking dish over apples to serve.

Makes 4 servings

Spelt Apple Betty

Ingredients:
¾ cup xylitol or turbinado sugar (sugar) (see glossary for definition)
Pinch of salt
1 teaspoon ground cinnamon
¼ teaspoon ground nutmeg
¼ teaspoon ground cloves
1 teaspoon fresh lemon peel, grated
1½ cups ground toasted spelt flakes
¼ cup butter
4 medium apples, peeled, cored, and thinly sliced
juice of 1 lemon
2 tablespoons apple juice

Directions:
Preheat the oven to 350°F. Coat an 8-inch square baking pan with canola cooking spray, and set aside.

Combine xylitol or turbinado sugar, salt, cinnamon, nutmeg, cloves, and lemon peel in 1-quart bowl. Set aside.

Place the spelt flakes and butter in a 1-quart bowl, and, using both hands, work the ingredients together until thoroughly mixed.

To assemble the dessert, place a third of the spelt flake mixture in the prepared pan, and pat the mixture over the bottom of the pan. Arrange half of the apple slices over the flake mixture. Sprinkle half of the sugar mixture over the apples, and sprinkle half of the lemon juice and half of the apple juice over the sugar. Repeat the layers, ending with the third layer of spelt flake mixture.

Cover the baking pan with aluminum foil, and bake for 40 minutes. Increase the heat to 400°F, remove the foil, and bake for an additional 10 minutes. Spoon the dessert into individual dishes, and serve warm.

Makes 6 servings

Apple-Cinnamon Rice Pudding

Ingredients:
1½ cups water
¾ cup short-grain rice, such as Arborio
½ teaspoon salt
3 cups 1% milk, divided
2 large egg yolks
¼ cup pure maple syrup
2 tablespoons brown sugar
1 teaspoon vanilla extract
2 tart apples, such as Granny Smith
1 teaspoon lemon juice
½ cup raisins
ground cinnamon for garnish

Directions:
Preheat oven to 350°F. Coat an 8-inch square baking dish with canola cooking spray.

Bring water to a boil in a 2-quart saucepan. Add rice and salt. Reduce heat to low and simmer, uncovered, stirring occasionally, until water is absorbed, 10 to 12 minutes.

Add 2 cups milk to rice and simmer, stirring occasionally, for 8 minutes. (Discard any skin that forms on the surface.) Remove from the heat.

Whisk remaining 1 cup milk, egg yolks, maple syrup, brown sugar, and vanilla in a medium bowl until smooth.

Peel and coarsely grate apples. Place in a small bowl and toss with lemon juice.

Stirring constantly, add about 1 cup hot rice mixture to the egg mixture. Scrape back into remaining rice mixture, stirring constantly. Add raisins and grated apples.

Scrape mixture into prepared baking dish. Place dish in a shallow roasting pan and pour enough simmering water into roasting pan to come halfway up the sides of the baking dish.

Bake pudding for 35 to 40 minutes, or until barely set. Serve warm or chilled, dusted with cinnamon.

Makes 6 servings

Baked Bananas

Ingredients:

4 (12-inch) pieces aluminum foil
4 large ripe bananas, peeled, split lengthwise, then halved
¼ cup no sugar apricot fruit jelly
1 teaspoon vanilla extract
1 teaspoon rum extract, optional
½ teaspoon ground cinnamon
½ teaspoon salt

Directions:

Position a rack in the center of the oven and preheat the oven to 500°F.

Lay the pieces of aluminum foil on a work surface, place one quartered banana on each piece, and top with 1 tablespoon fruit jelly, ¼ teaspoon vanilla, ¼ teaspoon rum extract (optional), teaspoon cinnamon, and teaspoon salt. Seal the packets and transfer them to a large rimmed baking sheet.

Bake until soft, about 10 minutes. Place the packets on 4 serving plates and let stand, sealed, at room temperature for 3 minutes before serving. Make sure you help any children open their packets because the escaping steam can be very hot.

Makes 4 servings

Banana-Maple Sorbet

Ingredients:
4 very ripe medium bananas
⅓ cup maple syrup
1 teaspoon vanilla extract
pinch of salt

Directions:
Peel bananas and place in large self-sealing plastic bag; freeze overnight or until very firm.

Slice frozen bananas. In a food processor or blender with knife blade attached, process bananas, syrup, vanilla and salt until creamy, about 2 minutes. Serve immediately.

Makes about 3 cups or 6 servings

Banana Pudding

Ingredients:
2 cups 2% milk
3 tablespoons cornstarch
3 eggs
1 tablespoon water
1 teaspoon vanilla
12 drops stevia (sugar) (see glossary for definition)
1 tablespoon fructose
1 tablespoon butter
6 bananas, peeled and sliced

Directions:
Heat milk in a heavy saucepan.

While milk is heating, separate eggs. To the yolks, add fructose, cornstarch and water. Slowly add yolk mixture to hot milk, stirring constantly. Bring up to a boil and boil just for a minute. Add vanilla and butter.

Cool for 15 minutes. Add stevia.

Cool and serve in a bowl over sliced bananas.

Makes 6-8 servings

Cherry-Blueberry Crisp

Ingredients:

⅓ cup brown sugar, firmly packed
2 tablespoons spelt flour (see glossary for definition)
½ teaspoon ground cinnamon
3 cups fresh Bing or other dark sweet cherries, pitted
2 cups fresh blueberries
1 tablespoon lemon juice
1 cup quick-cooking rolled oats
¼ cup brown sugar, firmly packed
¼ teaspoon ground cinnamon
¼ teaspoon ground ginger
3 tablespoons butter, melted

Directions:

In a shallow 2-quart casserole, stir together the ⅓ cup sugar, flour, and cinnamon. Add cherries, blueberries, and lemon juice; mix gently to coat fruit with sugar mixture. Spread out fruit mixture in an even layer.

In a small bowl, combine oats, the ¼ cup sugar, cinnamon, and ginger; add butter and stir with a fork until mixture is crumbly. Sprinkle mixture evenly over fruit.

Set casserole in a larger baking pan to catch any drips. Bake in a 350°F oven until fruit mixture is bubbly in center and topping is golden brown (35 to 40 minutes); if topping begins to darken excessively, cover it with foil. Serve hot, warm, or at room temperature. To serve, spoon into bowls.

Makes 6 servings

Maple-Pumpkin Custards

Ingredients:
1½ cups 1% milk
4 large eggs
¾ cup maple syrup
¾ cup canned unseasoned pumpkin purée
1 teaspoon ground cinnamon
½ teaspoon ground nutmeg
¼ teaspoon salt
3 tablespoons whipped cream

Directions:
Preheat oven to 325°F. Put a kettle of water on to heat for the water bath. Line a roasting pan with a folded kitchen towel.

Heat milk over low heat in a small saucepan until barely steaming but not boiling.

Whisk eggs and syrup in a large bowl until smooth. Gently whisk in the warm milk (a little bit at a time so the eggs don't cook). Add pumpkin purée, cinnamon, nutmeg and salt; whisk until blended.

Divide the mixture among six 6-ounce (¾ cup) custard cups. Skim foam from the surface. Place custard cups in the prepared roasting pan. Pour enough boiling water into the pan to come halfway up the sides of the custard cups. Place the pan in the oven and bake, uncovered, until custards are just set but still quiver in the center when shaken, 45 to 50 minutes. Transfer custards to a wire rack and let cool for 45 minutes. Cover and refrigerate for at least 1 hour, or until chilled.

To serve, top each custard with a spoonful of whipped cream.

Makes 6 servings

Fruit & Yogurt Parfaits

Ingredients:
two 8 ounce containers vanilla yogurt
2 cups fresh fruit (strawberries (1 pint) **or** strawberries and blueberries (1 cup strawberries and 1 cup blueberries) **or** peaches and berries (1 cup diced peaches and 1 cup berries) **or** mango and banana (1 cup diced mango and 1 cup thinly sliced banana).
almonds, sliced and toasted **or** low-fat granola for topping

Directions:
Use 4 parfait dishes or medium-size glass tumblers will work. For each serving, layer ¼ cup each of yogurt and fruit in the parfait dish; repeat each layer, then do the same for the other parfaits.

Sprinkle with topping of choice and serve.

Makes 4 servings

Lemon Cookies

Ingredients:
2½ cups whole-wheat spelt flour
1 teaspoon baking powder
1 teaspoon baking soda
½ teaspoon salt
1¼ cups turbinado sugar
½ cup unsweetened applesauce
¼ cup canola oil
4 teaspoons lemon zest, freshly grated
2 tablespoons fresh lemon juice

Directions:
Whisk flour, baking powder, baking soda and salt in a large bowl.

Whisk 1 cup turbinado sugar, applesauce, canola oil, lemon zest and lemon juice in another bowl until smooth. Make a well in the dry ingredients and add wet ingredients. Stir until blended. Cover with plastic wrap and refrigerate until chilled, 30 minutes to 1 hour.

Preheat oven to 350°F. Coat 2 baking sheets with canola cooking spray.

Place remaining ¼ cup sugar in a small bowl. Using spelt floured hands, roll dough into 1½" balls. Roll balls in sugar to coat and place 2 inches apart on the prepared baking sheets.

Bake the cookies, one sheet at a time, until very lightly browned, 12 to 14 minutes. (The longer they bake, the crisper they become.) Cool on the baking sheet for 2 minutes, then transfer to wire racks to cool completely.

Makes about 2 dozen cookies

Maple Baked Pears

Ingredients:
4 to 5 medium firm pears
¼ cup maple syrup
cinnamon
¼ cup walnuts, finely chopped
vanilla yogurt, frozen

Directions:
Preheat the oven to 350°F.

Quarter the pears lengthwise, and remove the cores and stem ends. Cut each quarter in half lengthwise. Arrange in a 9 by 9-inch nonstick baking pan.

Drizzle the syrup over the pears, and sprinkle with a little cinnamon. Scatter the walnuts over the pears.

Bake until the pears are tender but not overcooked, 25 to 30 minutes. Stir the mixture well about 15 minutes into the baking time. Serve warm in shallow bowls or over frozen yogurt if desired.

Makes 4 servings

Oatmeal Cookies

Ingredients:
2 cups spelt flour
1¼ cups turbinado sugar
1 teaspoon baking powder
½ teaspoon baking soda
1 teaspoon cinnamon
3 cups rolled oats
1 cup raisins
1 cup canola oil
2 eggs (beaten)
½ cup 2% milk
¾ teaspoon stevia (sugar) (see glossary for definition)

Directions:
Combine all dry ingredients and mix. Stir stevia into milk. To dry ingredients add remaining ingredients and mix. Drop by the teaspoonful onto cookie sheet. Bake in hot oven at 400° F for 10 to 12 minutes.

Makes approximately 2-3 dozen cookies

Orange Pudding Parfaits

Ingredients:

3 tablespoons quick-cooking tapioca
⅓ cup xylitol (sugar) (see glossary for definition)
2 egg whites
2½ cups 2% milk
½ teaspoon vanilla
1 tablespoon fresh orange peel
1 tablespoon orange-flavored liqueur (optional)
2 large oranges

Directions:

In a 2 to 3 quart pan, stir together tapioca, xylitol, egg whites, and milk; let stand for 5 minutes. Then bring to a full boil over medium heat, stirring constantly. Remove from heat and stir in vanilla, orange peel, and liqueur (if using). Let cool, uncovered, stirring once after 20 minutes.

Using a sharp knife, cut peel and all white membrane from oranges; cut segments free and lift out. Layer cooled tapioca and orange segments in four 8-ounce parfait glasses. Cover and refrigerate until cold before serving. (about 4 hours).

Makes 4 servings

Orange-Banana-Nectarine Freeze

Ingredients:
2 oranges, peeled, seeded, and white skin removed
2 bananas, peeled and cut into chunks
2 nectarines, peeled, pitted, and sliced

Directions:
Place oranges, bananas, and nectarines in blender. Blend until smooth

Pour into a bowl and put into freezer.

Stir every 2 hours until frozen.

Serve in dishes as you would ice cream.

Makes 3-4 servings

Peach Cobbler

Ingredients: Filling
⅔ cup turbinado sugar
1 tablespoon instant vanilla pudding mix
3 cups skinned peach slices, fresh or canned (no sugar or light syrup)
1 tablespoon honey
2 tablespoons butter
1 teaspoon cinnamon

Ingredients: Crust
1½ cups white spelt flour
1 tablespoon baking powder
dash of salt
3 tablespoons butter
¼ cup 2% milk

Directions: Filling
Preheat the oven to 425°F. Coat an 8-inch baking pan with canola cooking spray. Generously sprinkle with turbinado sugar. Set aside.

Combine the sugar and pudding mix in a 2-quart saucepan. Add the peaches and honey, and, stirring constantly, cook over low heat for about 5 minutes or until fruit is tender.

Pour the peach mixture into the prepared pan. Dot the top with the butter and sprinkle with the cinnamon. Set aside.

Directions: Crust
To make the crust, sift the flour, baking powder, and salt into a 2-quart bowl. Using your fingertips, pinch the butter into the flour until it is well distributed. Then stir in just enough of the milk to form a soft dough.

Transfer the dough to a spelt floured board, and knead for a few minutes, or until the dough is pliable. Using a lightly floured rolling pin, roll the dough into a ¼-inch thick 8-inch square. Transfer the square of dough to the pan, placing it over the peach mixture. Using a sharp knife, cut several slits in the dough to allow steam to escape during baking.

Bake for 25 to 30 minutes. Spoon into individual dessert dishes, and serve warm.

Makes 6 servings

Peach Shortcakes

Ingredients:
1 cup white spelt flour
2 teaspoons baking powder
¼ teaspoon baking soda
3 tablespoons butter
⅓ cup low-fat buttermilk
1 cup low-fat cottage cheese
about 3 tablespoons honey
⅛ teaspoon ground nutmeg
2 large firm-ripe peaches

Directions:
In a medium-size bowl, stir together spelt flour, baking powder, and baking soda until well blended. Using a blender or your fingers, cut in or rub in butter until mixture resembles coarse meal. Add buttermilk and stir just until dry ingredients are evenly moistened.

Turn dough out onto a lightly spelt floured board and knead gently just until smooth (about 1 minute). Divide dough into fourths. Pat each portion into a 3-inch-diameter round; place rounds well apart on an ungreased baking sheet.

Bake in a 450°F oven until lightly browned (about 15 minutes). Transfer to a rack and let cool slightly.

Meanwhile, whirl cottage cheese, 3 tablespoons of honey, and nutmeg in a blender or food processor until smooth. Peel, then pit and slice peaches.

To serve, split each biscuit in half horizontally. Set bottom halves on 4 plates; top each with a fourth of the cottage cheese mixture and a fourth of the peach slices. Cover lightly with biscuit tops. Serve with additional honey, if desired.

Makes 4 servings

Pie Crust

Ingredients:
2 cups white spelt flour
¼ teaspoon salt
⅓ cup canola oil
2-3 tablespoons cold water

Directions:
Mix all ingredients together with food processor or by hand.

Roll out between 2 pieces of wax paper in a 9" circle.

Remove top wax paper. Place pie pan upside down on top of crust and flip back over holding crust in place and center. Peel off wax paper and shape crust and edge.

Makes 1 pie crust shell

Pumpkin Custard

Ingredients:
1½ cups solid-packed canned pumpkin (not pumpkin pie filling)
1 cup fat-free evaporated milk
2 eggs
½ cup maple syrup
¼ cup xylitol (sugar) (see glossary for definition)
2 tablespoons powdered dry milk
2 teaspoons vanilla extract
1 teaspoon pumpkin pie spice

Directions:
Position a rack in the center of the oven and preheat the oven to 350°F.

Combine all the ingredients in a large bowl and whisk until smooth and creamy. Divide the mixture equally among 6 oven-safe, 1 cup ramekins (custard cups).

Place the filled ramekins on a baking sheet and bake until puffed and set, about 35 minutes. (The custards will still jiggle a little when shaken.) Cool on a wire rack at least 15 minutes before serving. The custards can be stored, covered, in the refrigerator up to 2 days.

Makes 6 servings

Ricotta-Pistachio Frozen Yogurt

Ingredients:
2 tablespoons pistachios, coarsely chopped
1½ cups part-skim ricotta cheese
1½ cups plain yogurt
14-ounce can nonfat sweetened condensed milk (not evaporated milk)
2 teaspoons vanilla extract
¼ teaspoon almond extract
¼ teaspoon ground nutmeg

Directions:
Chop pistachios or purchase already chopped. Toast pistachios in a small dry skillet over low heat, stirring constantly, until fragrant, about 5 minutes. Transfer to a plate to cool.

Process ricotta cheese in a food processor or blender until very smooth and creamy, 2 to 3 minutes. Add yogurt, sweetened condensed milk, vanilla, and almond extract and nutmeg. Process until smooth.

Pour ricotta mixture into an ice cream maker and freeze according to manufacturer's directions. Stir in pistachios.

Serve immediately or transfer to a storage container and let harden in the freezer for 1 to 1½ hours. Serve in chilled dishes.

Makes 10 servings, ½ cup each (1¼ quarts)

Trail Mix Bars

Ingredients:

1 cup white spelt flour
1 teaspoon baking powder
¾ cup dark raisins
¾ cup golden raisins
⅓ cup butter, at room temperature
½ cup firmly packed brown sugar
½ cup smooth unsweetened applesauce
2 large egg whites
2 teaspoons vanilla

Directions:

In a small bowl, stir together spelt flour, baking powder, and golden and dark raisins. In a food processor or large bowl, combine butter, sugar, applesauce, egg whites, and vanilla; whirl or beat with an electric mixer until smoothly blended. Add spelt flour mixture; whirl or beat until dry ingredients are evenly moistened. Spread batter in a lightly greased square 8-inch baking pan.

Bake in a 325°F oven until cookie is golden around edges and a wooden toothpick inserted in center comes out clean (about 40 minutes). Let cool in pan on a rack. To serve, cut into 2 inch squares.

Makes 16 bars

Vanilla Pudding

Ingredients:
2 cups 2% milk
1 tablespoon cornstarch
2 egg yolks
½ teaspoon stevia (sugar) (see glossary for definition)
1 tablespoon vanilla
½ teaspoon salt

Directions:
Beat egg yolks in a cup. Add ¼ cup milk to egg yolks and mix together. Add cornstarch to egg mixture and blend.

Pour this mixture along with salt and remaining milk into a saucepan. Heat on low heat stirring constantly until bubbly and thick.

Remove from heat and add vanilla and stevia.

Serve warm or cool.

Makes 4 servings

Watermelon Slush

Ingredients:
½ cup xylitol (sugar) (see glossary for definition)
¾ cup water
6 cups watermelon chunks, seeded
2 tablespoons lime juice, fresh

Directions:
Combine xylitol and water in a medium saucepan. Bring to a boil over medium-high heat, stirring to dissolve the sugar. Reduce the heat to low and simmer for 5 minutes. Remove from heat and let cool at room temperature, about 45 minutes. Cover and refrigerate until chilled, about 1 hour.

Place watermelon and lime juice in a food processor, blender, or slushy machine; process until smooth. Set a sieve over a large bowl and press the purée through to remove tiny seeds. Whisk in the sugar syrup.

Pour the watermelon mixture into a shallow metal pan and freeze until ice crystals form around the edge, about 30 minutes. Stir the ice crystals into the center of the pan and return to the freezer; repeat every 20 minutes until all the liquid is frozen.

Serve immediately or transfer to a storage container and let harden in the freezer for 1 to 1½ hours. Serve in chilled dishes.

Makes 12 servings, ½ cup each

Natural Sugar & Flour Substitutes

Granulated Sugar Substitutes: Definitions

Honey: Honey is a simple sugar, primarily glucose. Raw honey contains one of the highest enzyme contents. There are many types of honey including buckwheat, sage, orange blossom, etc.

Maple Syrup: Maple syrup is made from boiling down sap from the maple tree. It is a simple sugar. Maple syrup is wonderful for cooking because it adds such a delightful flavor.

Molasses: Molasses is formed when the liquid is spun out of cane sugar during processing. Molasses contains water, sucrose, ash, iron, vitamin B6, calcium and potassium.

Stevia: Stevia comes from an herb and is almost 10-15 times sweeter than regular sugar. Diabetics use stevia because research has shown stevia may actually lower blood sugar levels.

Turbinado: Turbinado comes from molasses when it is first separated. It is identical to white sugar in the way it is absorbed.

Xylitol: Xylitol is a natural type of sugar found in berries and birch bark. It doesn't spike blood sugar levels like regular sugar, has a low glycemic index, and researchers have found it safe for diabetics. It has actually been proven to prevent cavities.

Bleached White & Wheat Flour Substitutes: Definitions

Corn Flour: Corn flour is made from whole kernels of corn. The corn is finely ground. It is very good to use for breading for meats and vegetables.

Kamut Flour: The Kamut grain contains more protein, lipids and measures higher in 88% more minerals than found in the common wheat. Kamut contains gluten. Kamut has a buttery taste and is much higher in nutritional value than most other grains. Kamut flour can be used for almost all baking needs, just know that baked goods will come out browner.

Oat Flour: If you have high cholesterol or high blood sugar, oat flour can be a healthy substitute for you. It has been found to lower cholesterol, regulate blood sugar, reduce chances of getting certain cancers and push poisonous wastes through your system fast. Oat flour seems to add more moisture to cakes and breads, making it somewhat heavier but healthier.

Spelt Flour: Spelt flour is easily digested so it is very good for those of us who suffer with digestive problems. This grain is very disease resistant and has its own covering called a husk. The husk must be removed before using but you will purchase it already husked. It has a buttery flavor. It can be used in place of wheat flour in cooking and baking. Spelt is a wonderful flour substitute for bleached white baking flour.

Proportion Equal Measurements:

	To Replace 1 Cup Sugar	Liquid Reduction
Honey (bees)	½ cup	¼ cup
Maple Syrup (maple trees)	½-⅓ cup	*****
Molasses (sugar cane)	½ cup	¼ cup
Stevia (herb)	1-1½ tablespoon	*****
Turbinato (sugar cane)	1 cup	*****
Xylitol (berries & birch bark)	1 cup	*****

White & Wheat Bleached Flour Substitutes:

	To replace 1 cup bleached whole wheat or bleached white flour use:
Corn Flour	¾ cup
Kamut Flour	1 cup
Oat Flour	1⅓ cup
Spelt Flour (white or wheat)	1 cup

Bibliography

Arnold, D. "Best of all may be xylitol." The Doctors' Complete Booklet of Unbiased Breakthroughs. The Institute of Cooperative Medicine 1: 19, 2005.

Cheney, P. "Fibromyalgia Information, Diet & Nutritional Supplement Recommendations from Leading Doctors," ProHealth 5: 304, 2005.

Elrod, J.M. & Moeller, M. The Fibromyalgia Nutrition Guide. Utah: Woodland Publishing, 1999.

Smith, S.A. The Fibromyalgia Cookbook. Tennessee. Cumberland House Publishing, Inc., 2002.